· TREASURY OF ·
Cookies & Brownies

PUBLICATIONS INTERNATIONAL, LTD.

Cover photography by Sanders Studios, Inc., Chicago.

Pictured on the front cover: Tropical Sun Bars *(page 46)*, Strawberry Streusel Bars *(page 50)*, Raspberry Freckles *(page 102)*, Brownie Kiss Cups *(page 142)*, Yogurt Brownies *(page 130)*, Jam-up Oatmeal Cookies *(page 211)*, Watermelon Slices *(page 228)*, Pinwheel Cookies *(page 218)*, Chocolate-Dipped Brandy Snaps *(page 206)*, Two-Toned Spritz Cookies *(page 224)*, Black and White Cut-Outs *(page 212)*, Original Toll House® Chocolate Chip Cookies *(page 16)*, Chocolate Sugar Cookies *(page 188)* and Peanut Butter Sensations *(page 182)*.

Pictured on the opposite page *(top to bottom):* Black Forest Oatmeal Fancies *(page 30)*, Checkerboard Bars *(page 226)* and Sour Cream Walnut Brownies *(page 126)*.

ISBN: 0-7853-0797-4

Library of Congress Catalog Card Number: 95-68462

Manufactured in U.S.A.

8 7 6 5 4 3 2 1

Microwave Cooking: Microwave ovens vary in wattage. The cooking times given in this publication are approximate. Use the cooking times as guidelines and check for doneness before adding more time. Consult manufacturer's instructions for suitable microwave-safe cooking dishes.

Preparation/Cooking Times: The preparation times in this book are based on the average amount of time necessary to assemble the ingredients before baking, cooking, chilling, freezing or serving. These times do not include the advance preparation of some ingredients such as "chopped nuts." When appropriate, simultaneous preparations were taken into account. Preparation of optional ingredients is not included.

Contents

Cookie & Brownie Basics

There is nothing quite like the tantalizing aromas and luscious flavors of homemade cookies and brownies. These delightful recipes will help you discover, or rediscover, the many pleasures of preparing sweet treats for family and friends.

From melt-in-your-mouth cookies to delectable brownies, these easy-to-follow recipes are a delight to make, bake and eat. The following guidelines are chock-full of tips and hints for successful cookie and brownie baking. Be sure to read this section before you begin. Even the most accomplished bakers will discover helpful tips to make their time in the kitchen easier and more enjoyable.

Combine this helpful information with over 250 kitchen-tested recipes developed by your favorite brand name food companies, and you have an impressive collection of cookie and brownie recipes to treasure for years to come.

General Guidelines

Take the guesswork out of cookie baking by practicing the following techniques.
• Read the entire recipe before beginning to be sure you have all the necessary ingredients and utensils.

• Remove butter, margarine and cream cheese from the refrigerator to soften, if necessary.

• Toast, chop and grind nuts, peel and slice fruit, and melt chocolate before preparing the cookie dough.

• Measure all the ingredients accurately and assemble them in the order they are listed in the recipe.

• When making bar cookies or brownies, use the pan size specified in the recipe. Prepare the pans according to the recipe directions.

• Adjust oven racks and preheat the oven. Check oven temperature for accuracy with an oven thermometer.

• Follow recipe directions and baking times exactly. Check for doneness using the test given in the recipe.

Measuring Ingredients

Dry Ingredients: Always use standardized measuring spoons and cups. Fill the appropriate measuring spoon or cup to overflowing and level it off with a metal spatula or flat edge of a knife. When

measuring flour, lightly spoon it into the measuring cup and then level it off. Do not tap or bang the measuring cup since this will pack the flour. If a recipe calls for "sifted flour," sift the flour before it is measured. If a recipe calls for "flour, sifted," measure the flour first then sift.

Liquid Ingredients: Use a standardized glass or plastic measuring cup with a pouring spout. Place the cup on a flat surface, fill to the desired mark and check the measurement at eye level. When measuring sticky liquids, such as honey and molasses, grease the measuring cup or spray it with nonstick cooking spray before filling; this assures that the sticky substance won't cling.

Melting Chocolate

Make sure the utensils used for melting chocolate are completely dry. Moisture causes chocolate to "seize," which means it becomes stiff and grainy. If this happens, add ½ teaspoon shortening (not butter) for each ounce of chocolate and stir until smooth. Chocolate scorches easily, and once scorched cannot be used. Follow one of these three methods for successful melting:

Double Boiler: This is the safest method because it prevents scorching. Place the chocolate in the top of a double boiler or in a heatproof bowl over hot, not boiling, water; stir until smooth. (Make sure that the water remains just below a simmer and is one inch below the bottom of the top pan). Be careful that no steam or water gets into the chocolate.

Direct Heat: Place the chocolate in a heavy saucepan and melt over very low heat, stirring constantly. Remove the chocolate from heat as soon as it is melted. Be sure to watch the chocolate carefully because it is easily scorched when using this method.

Microwave Oven: Place an unwrapped 1-ounce square or 1 cup of chips in a small microwavable bowl. Microwave on HIGH 1 to 1½ minutes, stirring after 1 minute. Stir the chocolate at 30-second intervals until smooth. Be sure to stir microwaved chocolate since it may retain its original shape even when melted.

Toasting Nuts

Toasting nuts brings out their flavor and fragrance. Spread the nuts in a single layer on a rimmed baking sheet. Bake in a 325°F oven for 8 to 10 minutes or until golden. Stir the nuts occasionally during baking to ensure even toasting. The nuts will darken and become crisper as they cool. To toast a small amount of nuts, place them in a dry skillet over low heat. Stir constantly for 2 to 4 minutes or until the nuts darken slightly and are fragrant.

Toasting Coconut

Spread the flaked coconut in a thin layer on a rimmed baking sheet. Bake in a 325°F oven for 7 to 10 minutes. Shake the pan or stir the coconut occasionally during baking to promote even browning and prevent burning.

Tinting Coconut

Dilute a few drops of food coloring with ½ teaspoon milk or water in a small bowl. Add 1 to 1⅓ cups flaked coconut and toss with a fork until evenly tinted.

Preparation Tips

The seemingly endless variety of cookies can actually be divided into five basic types: bar, drop, refrigerator, rolled and shaped. These types are determined by the consistency of the dough and how it is formed into cookies.

Bar Cookies: Bar cookies and brownies are two of the easiest cookies to make. These cookies are also quick to prepare since they bake all at once rather than in several batches placed on a cookie sheet.

Always use the pan size specified in the recipe. Substituting a pan of a different size will affect the cookies' cooking time and texture. A smaller pan will cause the bars to become cakelike and a larger pan will produce a flatter bar with a drier texture.

Most bar cookies should cool in the pan set on a wire rack until barely warm before cutting into bars or squares. Try cutting bar cookies into triangles or diamonds for a festive new shape. To make serving easy, remove a corner piece first; then remove the rest.

Sprinkle bar cookies with powdered sugar for a simple garnish. Dress up frosted bar cookies by topping with nuts, chocolate chips or curls, or dried or candied fruit.

Drop Cookies: These cookies are named for the way they are formed. Spoonfuls of soft dough are dropped onto a cookie sheet and flatten during baking. Space dough about 2 inches apart on cookie sheets to allow for spreading unless the recipe directs otherwise.

Spoonfuls of dough that are uniform in size and shape will finish baking at the same time. To easily shape drop cookies, use an ice-cream scoop with a release bar. The bar usually has a number on it to indicate the number of scoops that can be made from one quart of ice cream. The handiest sizes for cookies are #80 or #90 scoops. They will yield about one rounded teaspoonful of dough for each cookie.

Refrigerator Cookies: Refrigerator doughs are perfect for advance preparation. Tightly wrapped rolls of dough can be stored in the refrigerator for up to one week or frozen for up to six weeks. These rich doughs are ready to be sliced and baked at a moment's notice.

Always shape the dough into rolls before chilling. Shaping is easier if you first place the dough on a piece of waxed paper or plastic wrap. If desired, you can gently press chopped nuts, flaked coconut or colored sugar into the roll. Before chilling, wrap the rolls securely in plastic wrap or air may penetrate the dough and cause it to dry out.

Use gentle pressure and a back-and-forth sawing motion when slicing the rolls so the cookies will keep their round shape. Rotating the roll while slicing also prevents one side from flattening.

Rolled Cookies: Rolled or cut-out cookies are made from stiff doughs that are rolled out and cut into fancy shapes with floured cookie cutters, a knife or a pastry wheel.

Chill the cookie dough before rolling for easier handling. Remove only enough dough from the refrigerator to work with at one time. Save any trimmings and reroll them all at once to prevent the dough from becoming tough.

To make your own custom-designed cookie cutters, cut a simple shape out of clean, heavy cardboard or poster board. Place the cardboard pattern on the rolled out dough and cut around it using a sharp knife.

Shaped Cookies: These cookies can be simply hand-shaped into balls or crescents, forced through a cookie press or pastry bag into more complex shapes, or baked in cookie molds.

By using different plates in a cookie press or different tips on a pastry bag, spritz cookies can be formed into many shapes. If your first efforts are not successful, just transfer the dough back to the cookie press or pastry bag and try again. The dough itself can be flavored or tinted with food coloring and the pressed shapes can be decorated before baking with colored sugar or candied fruit.

Baking

The best cookie sheets to use are those with little or no sides. They allow the heat to circulate easily during baking and promote even browning. Another way to promote even baking and browning is to place only one cookie sheet at a time in the center of the oven. If the cookies brown unevenly, rotate the cookie sheet from front to back halfway through the baking time. If you do use more than one sheet at a time, rotate the cookie sheets from the top to the bottom rack halfway through the baking time.

When a recipe calls for greased cookie sheets, use shortening or nonstick cooking spray for best results. Lining the cookie sheets with parchment paper is an alternative to greasing. It eliminates clean up, bakes cookies more evenly and allows them to cool right on the paper instead of on wire racks. Allow cookie sheets to cool between batches; the dough will spread if placed on a hot cookie sheet.

Most cookies bake quickly and should be watched carefully to avoid overbaking. Check them at the minimum baking time, then watch them carefully to make sure they don't burn. It is generally better to slightly underbake, rather than to overbake, cookies. Here are some guidelines that describe when different types of cookies are finished baking.

Cookie Baking Guidelines

Cookie Type	Doneness Test
Fudgelike Bar Cookies	Surface appears dull and slight imprint remains after touching surface with fingertip
Cakelike Bar Cookies	Wooden toothpick inserted into center comes out clean and dry
Drop Cookies	Lightly browned and slight imprint remains after touching surface with fingertip
Refrigerator Cookies	Edges are firm and bottoms are lightly browned
Rolled Cookies	Edges are firm and bottoms are lightly browned
Shaped Cookies	Edges are lightly browned

Most cookies should be removed from cookie sheets immediately after baking and placed in a single layer on wire racks to cool. Fragile cookies may need to cool slightly on the cookie sheet before being moved. Always cool cookies completely before stacking and storing. Bar cookies and brownies may be cooled and covered with foil or plastic wrap for storage in the baking pan.

Storing

Unbaked cookie dough can be refrigerated for up to one week or frozen for up to six weeks. Rolls of dough should be sealed tightly in plastic wrap; other doughs should be stored in airtight containers. Label dough or container with baking information for convenience.

Store soft and crisp cookies separately at room temperature to prevent changes in texture and flavor. Keep soft cookies in airtight containers. If they begin to dry out, add a piece of apple or bread to the container to help them retain moisture. Store crisp cookies in containers with loose-fitting lids to prevent moisture buildup. If they become soggy, heat undecorated cookies in a 300°F oven for 3 to 5 minutes to restore crispness.

Store cookies with sticky glazes, fragile decorations and icings in single layers between sheets of waxed paper. As a rule, crisp cookies freeze better than soft, moist cookies. Rich, buttery bar cookies and brownies are an exception to this rule since they freeze extremely well. Freeze baked cookies in airtight containers or freezer bags for up to six months. Thaw cookies and brownies unwrapped at room temperature. Meringue-based cookies do not freeze well and chocolate-dipped cookies may discolor if frozen for a long period of time.

Tips for Sending Cookies

Bake soft, moist cookies that can handle jostling rather than fragile, brittle cookies that might crumble. Brownies and bar cookies are generally sturdy, but avoid shipping those with moist fillings and frostings since they become sticky at room temperature. For the same reason, shipping anything with chocolate during the summer or to warm climates is also risky.

Wrap each type of cookie separately to retain flavors and textures. Cookies can also be wrapped back-to-back in pairs with either plastic wrap or foil. Bar cookies should be packed in layers, or they can be sent in a covered foil pan as long as the pan is well-cushioned inside the shipping box. Place wrapped cookies as tightly as possible in snug rows inside a sturdy shipping box or container.

Fill the bottom of the shipping container with an even layer of packing material. Do not use popped popcorn or puffed cereal as it may attract insects. Place crumbled waxed paper, newspaper or paper toweling between layers of wrapped cookies. Fill any crevices with packing material, and add a final layer at the top of the box. Ship the container to arrive as soon as possible.

Galaxy o'Chips

Orange-Walnut Chippers

½ cup butter or margarine, softened
1 cup packed light brown sugar
1 egg
1 tablespoon grated orange peel
½ cup all-purpose flour
¼ teaspoon baking soda
¼ teaspoon salt
1½ cups uncooked rolled oats
1 cup semisweet chocolate chips
½ cup coarsely chopped walnuts

Preheat oven to 375°F. Lightly grease cookie sheets; set aside.

Beat butter and sugar in large bowl until light and fluffy. Beat in egg and orange peel. Add flour, baking soda and salt to butter mixture. Beat until well blended. Stir in oats, chips and nuts. Drop by rounded teaspoonfuls 2 inches apart onto prepared cookie sheets.

Bake 10 to 12 minutes or until golden brown. Let cookies stand on cookie sheets 2 minutes. Remove cookies to wire racks; cool completely.

Makes about 3 dozen cookies

Double Nut Chocolate Chip Cookies

1 package DUNCAN HINES® Moist Deluxe
    Yellow Cake Mix
½ cup butter or margarine, melted
1 egg
1 cup semisweet chocolate chips
½ cup finely chopped pecans
1 cup sliced almonds, divided

1. Preheat oven to 375°F. Grease cookie sheets.

2. Combine cake mix, butter and egg in large bowl. Mix at low speed with electric mixer until just blended. Stir in chocolate chips, pecans and ¼ cup almonds. Shape rounded tablespoonfuls of dough into balls. Place remaining ¾ cup almonds in shallow bowl. Press tops of cookies in almonds. Place 1 inch apart on prepared cookie sheets.

3. Bake 9 to 11 minutes or until lightly browned. Cool 2 minutes on cookie sheets. Remove to cooling racks.

Makes 3 to 3½ dozen cookies

Double Chocolate Banana Cookies

3 to 4 extra-ripe, medium DOLE® Bananas,
    peeled
2 cups rolled oats
2 cups sugar
1¾ cups all-purpose flour
½ cup unsweetened cocoa powder
1 teaspoon baking soda
½ teaspoon salt
2 eggs, slightly beaten
1¼ cups margarine, melted
1 cup DOLE® Chopped Natural Almonds,
    toasted
2 cups semisweet chocolate chips

• Purée bananas in blender; measure 2 cups for recipe.

• Combine oats, sugar, flour, cocoa, baking soda and salt. Stir in bananas, eggs and margarine until blended. Stir in almonds and chocolate chips.

• Refrigerate batter 1 hour or until mixture becomes partially firm (batter runs during baking if too soft).

• Measure ¼ cup batter for each cookie; drop onto greased cookie sheets. Flatten slightly with spatula.

• Bake in 350°F oven 15 to 17 minutes or until cookies are golden brown. Remove to wire racks to cool.

Makes about 2½ dozen (3-inch) cookies

Prep Time: 15 minutes
Chill Time: 1 hour
Bake Time: 17 minutes each batch

Double Nut Chocolate Chip Cookies

Ivory Chip Strawberry Fudge Drops

⅔ BUTTER FLAVOR* CRISCO® Stick or ⅔ cup
    BUTTER FLAVOR* CRISCO® all-vegetable
    shortening
1 cup sugar
1 egg
½ teaspoon strawberry extract
½ cup buttermilk**
6 tablespoons puréed frozen sweetened
    strawberries
1¾ cups all-purpose flour
6 tablespoons unsweetened cocoa powder
¾ teaspoon baking soda
½ teaspoon salt
1½ cups white chocolate baking chips or white
    chocolate bar, cut into pieces

*Butter Flavor Crisco is artificially flavored.

**You may substitute 1½ teaspoons lemon juice or vinegar plus enough milk to make ½ cup for the buttermilk. Stir. Wait 5 minutes before using.

1. **Heat** oven to 350°F. **Grease** baking sheets with shortening. **Place** sheets of foil on countertop for cooling cookies.

2. **Combine** shortening, sugar, egg and strawberry extract in large bowl. **Beat** at medium speed of electric mixer until well blended. **Beat** in buttermilk and strawberry purée.

3. **Combine** flour, cocoa, baking soda and salt. **Mix** into shortening mixture at low speed of electric mixer until blended. **Stir** in white chocolate chips.

4. **Drop** by rounded tablespoonfuls 2 inches apart onto prepared baking sheets.

5. **Bake** one baking sheet at a time at 350°F for 11 to 12 minutes or until tops spring back when pressed lightly. *Do not overbake.* **Cool** 2 minutes on baking sheets. **Remove** cookies to foil to cool completely.

Makes about 2½ dozen cookies

San Francisco Cookies

2 extra-ripe, medium DOLE® Bananas, peeled
    and cut into chunks
2 cups granola
1½ cups all-purpose flour
1 cup packed brown sugar
1 teaspoon baking powder
1 teaspoon ground cinnamon
2 eggs
½ cup margarine, melted
¼ cup vegetable oil
1 cup semisweet chocolate chips

• Preheat oven to 350°F. Lightly grease cookie sheets. In blender or food processor, process bananas until puréed (1 cup).

• Combine granola, flour, sugar, baking powder and cinnamon in large bowl. Beat in puréed bananas, eggs, margarine and oil. Stir in chocolate chips.

• Drop by ¼ cupfuls onto prepared cookie sheets. Spread dough into 2½- to 3-inch circles. Bake about 16 minutes or until golden. Remove to wire racks to cool.

Makes about 16 cookies

Ivory Chip Strawberry Fudge Drops

Ultimate Chocolate Chip Cookies

1¼ cups firmly packed brown sugar
¾ BUTTER FLAVOR* CRISCO® Stick or ¾ cup
    BUTTER FLAVOR* CRISCO® all-vegetable
    shortening
2 tablespoons milk
1 tablespoon vanilla
1 egg
1¾ cups all-purpose flour
1 teaspoon salt
¾ teaspoon baking soda
1 cup semisweet chocolate chips
1 cup coarsely chopped pecans (optional)**

*Butter Flavor Crisco is artificially flavored.

**If nuts are omitted, add an additional ½ cup semisweet chocolate chips.

1. Heat oven to 375°F. **Place** sheets of foil on countertop for cooling cookies.

2. Combine brown sugar, shortening, milk and vanilla in large bowl. **Beat** at medium speed of electric mixer until well blended. **Beat** in egg.

3. Combine flour, salt and baking soda. **Mix** into shortening mixture just until blended. **Stir** in chocolate chips and pecan pieces.

4. Drop by rounded measuring tablespoonfuls 3 inches apart onto ungreased baking sheets.

5. Bake one baking sheet at a time at 375°F for 8 to 10 minutes for chewy cookies, or 11 to 13 minutes for crisp cookies. *Do not overbake.* **Cool** 2 minutes on baking sheets. **Remove** cookies to foil to cool completely.

Makes about 3 dozen cookies

Almond Double Chip Cookies

¾ cup butter or margarine, softened
¾ cup packed light brown sugar
1 egg
½ teaspoon almond extract
1½ cups all-purpose flour
¼ teaspoon baking soda
    Dash salt
1 cup (6 ounces) semisweet chocolate chips
1 cup (6 ounces) vanilla milk chips
½ cup slivered blanched almonds

Preheat oven to 375°F. Line cookie sheets with parchment paper or leave ungreased.

Beat butter and brown sugar in large bowl with electric mixer until creamy. Beat in egg and almond extract.

Combine flour, baking soda and salt in small bowl; blend into butter mixture. Stir in semisweet and vanilla milk chips and almonds. Drop by rounded tablespoonfuls, 3 inches apart, onto prepared cookie sheets. Bake 8 to 10 minutes or until lightly browned. *Do not overbake.* Cool 2 minutes on cookie sheets; remove to wire racks to cool completely.

Makes about 3 dozen cookies

Double Chocolate Chip Cookies

2 cups all-purpose flour
1 teaspoon baking soda
½ teaspoon salt
4 cups (24-ounce package) HERSHEY®S
    Semi-Sweet Chocolate Chips, divided
¾ cup (1½ sticks) butter or margarine,
    softened
¾ cup sugar
2 eggs

Heat oven to 350°F. In small bowl, stir together flour, baking soda and salt.

In medium microwave-safe bowl, place 2 cups chocolate chips. Microwave at HIGH (100% power) 1½ minutes; stir. Microwave at HIGH (100% power) an additional 30 seconds or until chips are melted and smooth when stirred; cool slightly.

In large bowl, beat butter and sugar until light and fluffy. Add eggs; beat well. Blend in melted chocolate. Gradually add flour mixture to chocolate mixture, beating well. Stir in remaining 2 cups chips. Drop dough by rounded teaspoonfuls onto ungreased cookie sheets.

Bake 8 to 9 minutes. *Do not overbake.* Cookies should be soft. Cool slightly. Remove from cookie sheets to wire racks; cool completely. *Makes about 5 dozen cookies*

Top to bottom: Double Chocolate Chip Cookies and Forgotten Chips Cookies (page 30)

Original Toll House® Chocolate Chip Cookies

2¼ cups all-purpose flour
1 teaspoon baking soda
1 teaspoon salt
1 cup (2 sticks) butter, softened
¾ cup granulated sugar
¾ cup packed brown sugar
1 teaspoon vanilla extract
2 eggs
2 cups (12-ounce package) NESTLÉ® Toll House® Semi-Sweet Chocolate Morsels
1 cup nuts, chopped

Preheat oven to 375°F. In small bowl, combine flour, baking soda and salt; set aside.

In large bowl, beat butter, granulated sugar, brown sugar and vanilla extract until creamy. Beat in eggs. Gradually beat in flour mixture. Stir in morsels and nuts. Drop by rounded measuring tablespoonfuls onto ungreased cookie sheets.

Bake 9 to 11 minutes or until edges are golden brown. Let stand on cookie sheets 2 minutes. Remove from cookie sheets; cool completely on wire racks.

Makes about 5 dozen cookies

Pan Cookies: Preheat oven to 375°F. Prepare dough as directed above. Spread dough in greased 15½×10½×1-inch jelly-roll pan. Bake 20 to 25 minutes. Cool completely in pan on wire rack. Cut into 2-inch squares. Makes about 35 squares.

Giant Toll House® Cookies: Preheat oven to 375°F. Prepare dough as directed above. Drop by ¼ cupfuls onto ungreased cookie sheets. Press lightly into 3-inch circles. Bake 10 to 12 minutes or until edges are golden brown. Let stand on cookie sheets 2 minutes. Remove from cookie sheets; cool completely on wire racks. Makes about 20 (4-inch) cookies.

Double Chocolate Cookies

2 cups biscuit baking mix
1 (14-ounce) can EAGLE® Brand Sweetened Condensed Milk (NOT evaporated milk)
8 (1-ounce) squares semisweet chocolate *or* 1 (12-ounce) package semisweet chocolate chips, melted
3 tablespoons margarine or butter, melted
1 egg
1 teaspoon vanilla extract
6 (1¼-ounce) white candy bars with almonds, broken into small pieces
¾ cup chopped nuts

Preheat oven to 350°F. In large mixer bowl, combine all ingredients except candy pieces and nuts; beat until smooth. Stir in remaining ingredients. Drop by rounded teaspoonfuls, 2 inches apart, onto ungreased cookie sheets.

Bake 10 minutes or until tops are slightly crusted (*do not overbake*). Cool on wire racks. Store tightly covered at room temperature. *Makes 4½ dozen cookies*

Mint Chocolate Cookies: Omit white candy bars. Stir in ¾ cup mint-flavored chocolate chips. Proceed as above.

Original Toll House® Chocolate Chip Cookies

Chocolate Chip Chewies

1¼ cups firmly packed light brown sugar
 ¾ BUTTER FLAVOR* CRISCO® Stick or ¾ cup
    BUTTER FLAVOR* CRISCO® all-vegetable
    shortening
 2 tablespoons milk
 1 tablespoon vanilla
 1 egg
1¾ cups all-purpose flour
 1 teaspoon salt
 ¾ teaspoon baking soda
 1 cup coarsely chopped pecans
 1 cup quick oats, uncooked
 1 cup semisweet chocolate chips
 ⅓ cup flake coconut

*Butter Flavor Crisco is artificially flavored.

1. Heat oven to 375°F. **Place** sheets of foil on countertop for cooling cookies.

2. Combine brown sugar, shortening, milk and vanilla in large bowl. **Beat** at medium speed of electric mixer until well blended. **Beat** egg into shortening mixture.

3. Combine flour, salt and baking soda. **Mix** into shortening mixture just until blended. **Stir** in pecans, oats, chocolate chips and coconut.

4. Drop by rounded measuring tablespoonfuls of dough 3 inches apart onto ungreased baking sheets.

5. Bake one baking sheet at a time at 375°F for 8 to 10 minutes for chewy cookies, or 11 to 13 minutes for crisp cookies. *Do not overbake.* **Cool** 2 minutes on baking sheets. **Remove** cookies to foil to cool completely.

Makes 4 dozen cookies

Ultimate Chippers

2½ cups all-purpose flour
 1 teaspoon baking soda
 ½ teaspoon salt
 1 cup butter or margarine, softened
 1 cup packed light brown sugar
 ½ cup granulated sugar
 2 eggs
 1 tablespoon vanilla
 1 cup semisweet chocolate chips
 1 cup milk chocolate chips
 1 cup vanilla milk chips
 ½ cup coarsely chopped pecans (optional)

Preheat oven to 375°F. Combine flour, baking soda and salt in medium bowl.

Beat butter, brown sugar and granulated sugar in large bowl until light and fluffy. Beat in eggs and vanilla. Add flour mixture to butter mixture; beat until well blended. Stir in chips and pecans.

Drop by heaping teaspoonfuls 2 inches apart onto ungreased cookie sheets. Bake 10 to 12 minutes or until edges are golden brown. Let cookies stand on cookie sheets 2 minutes. Remove cookies to wire racks; cool completely.

Makes about 6 dozen cookies

Ultimate Chippers

Kids' Favorite Jumbo Chippers

Kids' Favorite Jumbo Chippers

    1 cup butter or margarine, softened
    ¾ cup granulated sugar
    ¾ cup packed brown sugar
    2 eggs
    1 teaspoon vanilla
2¼ cups all-purpose flour
    1 teaspoon baking soda
    ¾ teaspoon salt
    1 (9-ounce) package candy-coated chocolate
       pieces
    1 cup peanut butter flavored chips

Preheat oven to 375°F. Beat butter, granulated sugar and brown sugar in large bowl until light and fluffy. Beat in eggs and vanilla. Add flour, baking soda and salt. Beat until well blended. Stir in chocolate pieces. Drop by rounded tablespoonfuls 3 inches apart onto ungreased cookie sheets.

Bake 10 to 12 minutes or until edges are golden brown. Let cookies stand on cookie sheets 2 minutes. Remove cookies to wire racks; cool completely.   *Makes 3 dozen cookies*

Brownie Cookie Bites

1½ cups (9 ounces) NESTLÉ® Toll House®
     Semi-Sweet Chocolate Morsels, divided
1 tablespoon butter
¼ cup all-purpose flour
¼ teaspoon baking powder
1 egg
⅓ cup granulated sugar
½ teaspoon vanilla extract

Melt ½ cup morsels and butter over hot (not boiling) water, stirring until smooth. Combine flour and baking powder; set aside.

Beat egg and sugar in large mixer bowl at high speed, about 3 minutes or until mixture is thick. Stir in vanilla and melted chocolate mixture. Gradually blend in flour mixture. Stir in remaining 1 cup morsels. Drop by level tablespoons onto greased baking sheets.

Bake in preheated 350°F oven for 8 to 10 minutes or until cookies are puffed and tops are cracked and moist (cookies will look slightly underbaked). Let stand for 5 minutes. Remove from baking sheets; cool on wire racks.

Makes about 1½ dozen cookies

Crunchy Chocolate Chipsters

1¼ cup packed light brown sugar
¾ BUTTER FLAVOR* CRISCO® Stick or ¾ cup
     BUTTER FLAVOR* CRISCO® all-vegetable
     shortening
2 tablespoons milk
1 tablespoon vanilla
1 egg
1½ cups flour
1 teaspoon salt
¾ teaspoon baking soda
2 cups crispy rice cereal
1 cup semisweet miniature chocolate chips

*Butter Flavor Crisco is artificially flavored.

1. Heat oven to 375°F. **Place** sheets of foil on countertop for cooling cookies.

2. Combine brown sugar, shortening, milk and vanilla in large bowl. **Beat** at medium speed of electric mixer until well blended. **Beat** egg into shortening mixture.

3. Combine flour, salt and baking soda. **Mix** into shortening mixture just until blended. **Stir** in cereal and chocolate chips.

4. Drop by rounded tablespoonfuls 2 inches apart onto ungreased baking sheets.

5. Bake one baking sheet at a time at 375°F for 10 to 12 minutes. *Do not overbake.* **Cool** 2 minutes on baking sheets. **Remove** cookies to foil to cool completely.

Makes about 3 dozen cookies

Sour Cream Chocolate Chip Cookies

    1 BUTTER FLAVOR* CRISCO® Stick or 1 cup
        BUTTER FLAVOR* CRISCO® all-vegetable
        shortening
    1 cup packed brown sugar
    ½ cup granulated sugar
    1 egg
    ½ cup sour cream
    ¼ cup warm honey
    2 teaspoons vanilla
    2½ cups all-purpose flour
    1½ teaspoons baking powder
    ½ teaspoon salt
    2 cups semisweet or milk chocolate chips
    1 cup coarsely chopped walnuts

*Butter Flavor Crisco is artificially flavored.

1. Heat oven to 375°F. **Grease** baking sheets with shortening. **Place** sheets of foil on countertop for cooling cookies.

2. Combine shortening, brown sugar and granulated sugar in large bowl. **Beat** at medium speed of electric mixer until well blended. **Beat** in egg, sour cream, honey and vanilla. **Beat** until just blended.

3. Combine flour, baking powder and salt. **Mix** into shortening mixture at low speed until just blended. **Stir** in chocolate chips and nuts.

4. Drop slightly rounded measuring tablespoonfuls of dough 2 inches apart onto prepared baking sheets.

5. Bake one baking sheet at a time at 375°F for 10 to 12 minutes or until set. *Do not overbake.* **Cool** 2 minutes on baking sheets. **Remove** cookies to foil to cool completely.
Makes about 5 dozen cookies

HERSHEY'S More Chips Chocolate Chip Cookies

    1½ cups butter, softened
    1 cup granulated sugar
    1 cup packed light brown sugar
    3 eggs
    2 teaspoons vanilla extract
    3⅓ cups all-purpose flour
    1½ teaspoons baking soda
    ¾ teaspoon salt
    4 cups (24-ounce package) HERSHEY'S
        Semi-Sweet Chocolate Chips

Preheat oven to 375°F. In large bowl, beat butter, granulated sugar and brown sugar until creamy. Add eggs and vanilla; beat until light and fluffy.

In another large bowl, stir together flour, baking soda and salt; gradually beat into butter mixture. Stir in chocolate chips. Drop by rounded teaspoonfuls onto ungreased cookie sheets.

Bake 8 to 10 minutes or until lightly browned. Cool slightly; remove from cookie sheets to wire racks. Cool completely.
Makes about 7½ dozen cookies

Dreamy Chocolate Chip Cookies

1¼ cups firmly packed brown sugar
¾ BUTTER FLAVOR* CRISCO® Stick or ¾ cup
     BUTTER FLAVOR* CRISCO® all-vegetable
     shortening
3 eggs, lightly beaten
2 teaspoons vanilla
1 (4-ounce) package German sweet chocolate,
     melted, cooled
3 cups all-purpose flour
1 teaspoon baking soda
½ teaspoon salt
1 (11½-ounce) package milk chocolate chips
1 (10-ounce) package premium semisweet
     chocolate pieces
1 cup coarsely chopped macadamia nuts

* Butter Flavor Crisco is artificially flavored.

1. Heat oven to 375°F. **Place** sheets of foil on countertop for cooling cookies.

2. Combine brown sugar, shortening, eggs and vanilla in large bowl. **Beat** at low speed of electric mixer until blended. **Increase** speed to high. **Beat** 2 minutes. **Add** melted chocolate. **Mix** until well blended.

3. Combine flour, baking soda and salt. **Add** gradually to shortening mixture at low speed.

4. Stir in chocolate chips, chocolate pieces and nuts with spoon. **Drop** by rounded tablespoonfuls 3 inches apart onto ungreased baking sheets.

Dreamy Chocolate Chip Cookies

5. Bake one baking sheet at a time at 375°F for 9 to 11 minutes or until set. *Do not overbake.* **Cool** 2 minutes on baking sheets. **Remove** cookies to foil to cool completely.

Makes about 3 dozen cookies

Whole Grain Chippers

 1 cup butter or margarine, softened
 ⅔ cup granulated sugar
 1 cup packed light brown sugar
 2 eggs
 1 teaspoon baking soda
 1 teaspoon vanilla
 Pinch salt
 1 cup whole wheat flour
 1 cup all-purpose flour
 2 cups uncooked rolled oats
 1 package (12 ounces) semisweet chocolate chips
 1 cup sunflower seeds

Preheat oven to 375°F. Lightly grease cookie sheets or line with parchment paper.

Beat butter, sugars and eggs in large bowl until light and fluffy. Beat in baking soda, vanilla and salt. Blend in flours and oats to make a stiff dough. Stir in chocolate chips. Shape rounded teaspoonfuls of dough into balls; roll in sunflower seeds. Place 2 inches apart on prepared cookie sheets.

Bake 8 to 10 minutes or until firm. *Do not overbake.* Cool a few minutes on cookie sheets, then remove to wire racks to cool completely.   *Makes about 6 dozen cookies*

Chocolate Chip Chocolate Cookies

 ½ cup butter or margarine, softened
 1 cup sugar
 1 egg
 1 teaspoon vanilla
 1½ cups unsifted all-purpose flour
 ⅓ cup HERSHEY'S Cocoa
 ½ teaspoon baking soda
 ½ teaspoon salt
 ¼ cup milk
 1 cup HERSHEY'S Semi-Sweet Chocolate Chips

Heat oven to 375°F. In large bowl, beat butter, sugar, egg and vanilla until light and fluffy. Combine flour, cocoa, baking soda and salt; add alternately with milk to butter mixture, blending well. Stir in chocolate chips.

Drop dough by rounded teaspoonfuls onto ungreased cookie sheets. Bake 10 to 12 minutes or until almost set (*do not overbake*). Cool 1 minute. Remove from cookie sheets; cool completely on wire racks.   *Makes about 3½ dozen cookies*

Oatmeal Scotch Chippers

1¼ BUTTER FLAVOR* CRISCO® Sticks or
    1¼ cups BUTTER FLAVOR* CRISCO®
    all-vegetable shortening
1½ cups firmly packed brown sugar
  1 cup granulated sugar
  3 eggs
1¼ cups extra-crunchy peanut butter
4½ cups rolled oats
  2 teaspoons baking soda
  1 cup semisweet chocolate chips
  1 cup butterscotch-flavored chips
  1 cup chopped walnuts

*Butter Flavor Crisco is artificially flavored.

1. Heat oven to 350°F. **Place** foil on countertop for cooling cookies.

2. Combine shortening, brown sugar and granulated sugar in large bowl. **Beat** at medium speed of electric mixer until well blended. **Beat** in eggs. **Add** peanut butter. **Beat** until blended.

3. Combine oats and baking soda. **Stir** into shortening mixture with spoon. **Stir** in chocolate chips, butterscotch chips and nuts until blended.

4. Drop by rounded teaspoonfuls 2 inches apart onto ungreased baking sheets.

5. Bake one baking sheet at a time at 350°F for 10 to 11 minutes or until lightly browned. *Do not overbake.* **Cool** 2 minutes on baking sheets. **Remove** to foil to cool completely.
Makes about 6 dozen cookies

Oatmeal Scotch Chippers

Oatmeal Scotchies™

1¼ cups all-purpose flour
1 teaspoon baking soda
½ teaspoon salt
½ teaspoon ground cinnamon
1 cup (2 sticks) butter or margarine, softened
¾ cup granulated sugar
¾ cup packed brown sugar
2 eggs
1 teaspoon vanilla extract or grated peel of
    1 orange
3 cups quick or old-fashioned oats, uncooked
2 cups (12-ounce package) NESTLÉ® Toll
    House® Butterscotch Flavored Morsels

Combine flour, baking soda, salt and cinnamon in small bowl; set aside.

Beat butter, granulated sugar, brown sugar, eggs and vanilla in large bowl until creamy. Gradually add flour mixture to butter mixture. Stir in oats and morsels. Drop by rounded tablespoon onto ungreased baking sheets.

Bake in preheated 375°F oven for 7 to 8 minutes for chewy cookies, 9 to 10 minutes for crisp cookies. Let stand for 2 minutes; remove to wire racks to cool completely.
Makes about 4 dozen cookies

Bar Cookie Variation: Spread dough in greased 15× 10-inch jelly-roll pan. Bake in preheated 375°F oven for 18 to 22 minutes or until very lightly browned. Cool; cut into 2×1½-inch bars. Makes about 4 dozen bars.

Oatmeal Chocolate Chip Cookies

1 can (20 ounces) DOLE® Crushed Pineapple in
    Syrup or Juice
1½ cups brown sugar, packed
1 cup margarine, softened
1 egg
¼ teaspoon almond extract
4 cups rolled oats, uncooked
2 cups all-purpose flour
1 teaspoon baking powder
1 teaspoon salt
1 teaspoon ground cinnamon
½ teaspoon ground nutmeg
1 package (12 ounces) semisweet chocolate
    chips
¾ cup DOLE® Slivered Almonds, toasted
2 cups flaked coconut

● Preheat oven to 350°F. Grease cookie sheets. Drain pineapple well, reserving ½ cup liquid.

● In large bowl, beat brown sugar and margarine until light and fluffy. Beat in egg. Beat in pineapple, reserved ½ cup liquid and almond extract.

● In medium bowl, combine oats, flour, baking powder, salt, cinnamon and nutmeg. Add to margarine mixture; beat until blended. Stir in chocolate chips, almonds and coconut. Drop by heaping tablespoonfuls onto prepared cookie sheets. Flatten cookies slightly with back of spoon. Bake 20 to 25 minutes or until golden. Cool on wire racks.
Makes about 5 dozen cookies

Oatmeal Candied Chippers

¾ cup butter or margarine, softened
¾ cup granulated sugar
¾ cup packed light brown sugar
3 tablespoons milk
1 egg
2 teaspoons vanilla
¾ cup all-purpose flour
¾ teaspoon salt
½ teaspoon baking soda
3 cups uncooked rolled oats
1⅓ cups (10-ounce package) candy-coated
    semisweet chocolate chips or
    candy-coated chocolate pieces

Preheat oven to 375°F. Grease cookie sheets; set aside. Beat butter, granulated sugar and brown sugar in large bowl until light and fluffy. Add milk, egg and vanilla; beat well. Add flour, salt and baking soda. Beat until well combined. Stir in oats and chocolate chips.

Drop by rounded tablespoonfuls 2 inches apart on prepared cookie sheets. Bake 10 to 12 minutes or until edges are golden brown. Let cookies stand 2 minutes on cookie sheets. Remove cookies to wire racks; cool completely.

Makes about 4 dozen cookies

Chocolate Oatmeal Chippers

1¼ cups all-purpose flour
½ cup NESTLÉ® Toll House® Baking Cocoa
1 teaspoon baking soda
¼ teaspoon salt
1 cup (2 sticks) butter or margarine, softened
1 cup packed brown sugar
½ cup granulated sugar
1 teaspoon vanilla extract
2 eggs
2 cups (11½-ounce package) NESTLÉ® Toll
    House® Milk Chocolate Morsels
1¾ cups quick or old-fashioned oats, uncooked
1 cup chopped nuts (optional)

Combine flour, cocoa, baking soda and salt in medium bowl.

Beat butter, brown sugar, granulated sugar and vanilla in large bowl until creamy. Beat in eggs. Gradually beat in flour mixture. Stir in morsels, oats and nuts. Drop by rounded tablespoon onto ungreased baking sheets.

Bake in preheated 375°F oven for 9 to 12 minutes or until edges are set but centers are still soft. Let stand for 2 minutes; remove to wire racks to cool completely.

Makes about 4 dozen cookies

Bar Cookie Variation: Prepare dough as above. Spread into greased 15×10-inch jelly-roll pan. Bake in preheated 350°F oven for 25 to 30 minutes. Cool in pan on wire rack. Makes about 4 dozen bars.

Oatmeal Candied Chippers

Black Forest Oatmeal Fancies

1 BUTTER FLAVOR* CRISCO® Stick or 1 cup
    BUTTER FLAVOR* CRISCO® all-vegetable
    shortening
1 cup packed brown sugar
1 cup granulated sugar
2 eggs
2 teaspoons vanilla
1⅔ cups all-purpose flour
1 teaspoon baking soda
1 teaspoon salt
½ teaspoon baking powder
3 cups quick oats (not instant or old
    fashioned), uncooked
1 baking bar (6 ounces) white chocolate,
    coarsely chopped
6 squares (1 ounce each) semisweet chocolate,
    coarsely chopped
½ cup coarsely chopped red candied cherries
½ cup sliced almonds

*Butter Flavor Crisco is artificially flavored.

1. Heat oven to 375°F. **Place** sheets of foil on countertop for cooling cookies.

2. Combine shortening, brown sugar, granulated sugar, eggs and vanilla in large bowl. **Beat** at medium speed of electric mixer until well blended.

3. Combine flour, baking soda, salt and baking powder. **Mix** into shortening mixture at low speed until well blended. **Stir** in, one at a time, oats, white chocolate, semisweet chocolate, cherries and nuts with spoon.

4. Drop rounded tablespoonfuls of dough 2 inches apart onto ungreased baking sheets.

5. Bake one baking sheet at a time at 375°F for 9 to 11 minutes or until set. *Do not overbake.* **Cool** 2 minutes on baking sheets. **Remove** cookies to foil to cool completely.
Makes about 3 dozen cookies

Forgotten Chips Cookies

 2 egg whites
⅛ teaspoon cream of tartar
⅛ teaspoon salt
⅔ cup sugar
 1 teaspoon vanilla extract
 1 cup HERSHEY₍S Semi-Sweet Chocolate Chips
    or Milk Chocolate Chips

Heat oven to 375°F. Lightly grease cookie sheets. In small bowl, beat egg whites, cream of tartar and salt until soft peaks form. Gradually add sugar, beating until stiff peaks form. Carefully fold in vanilla extract and chocolate chips. Drop dough by teaspoonfuls onto prepared cookie sheets.

Place cookie sheets in preheated oven; immediately turn off oven and allow cookies to remain in oven six hours or overnight without opening door. Remove cookies from cookie sheets. Store in airtight container in cool, dry place.
Makes about 2½ dozen cookies

Brian's Buffalo Cookies

    1 BUTTER FLAVOR* CRISCO® Stick or 1 cup
        BUTTER FLAVOR* CRISCO® all-vegetable
        shortening, melted
    1 cup granulated sugar
    1 cup firmly packed brown sugar
    2 tablespoons milk
    1 teaspoon vanilla
    2 eggs
    2 cups all-purpose flour
    1 teaspoon baking powder
    1 teaspoon baking soda
    ½ teaspoon salt
    1 cup rolled oats (quick or old fashioned),
        uncooked
    1 cup cornflakes cereal, crushed to about
        ½ cup
    1 cup semisweet chocolate chips
    ½ cup chopped pecans
    ½ cup flake coconut

*Butter Flavor Crisco is artificially flavored.

1. Heat oven to 350°F. **Grease** baking sheets with shortening. **Place** sheets of foil on countertop for cooling cookies.

2. Combine shortening, granulated sugar, brown sugar, milk and vanilla in large bowl. **Beat** at low speed of electric mixer until well blended. **Add** eggs; beat at medium speed until well blended.

3. Combine flour, baking powder, baking soda and salt. **Add** gradually to shortening mixture at low speed. **Stir** in oats, cereal, chocolate chips, nuts and coconut. **Scoop** out about ¼ cupful of dough for each cookie. **Level** with knife. **Drop** 3 inches apart onto prepared baking sheets.

4. Bake one baking sheet at a time at 350°F for 13 to 15 minutes or until lightly browned around edges but still slightly soft in center. *Do not overbake.* **Cool** 3 minutes on baking sheets. **Remove** cookies to foil with wide, thin spatula.

Makes 2 to 2½ dozen cookies

Chocolate Chip 'n Oatmeal Cookies

    1 package (18.25 or 18.5 ounces) yellow cake
        mix
    1 cup rolled oats, uncooked
    ¾ cup butter or margarine, softened
    2 eggs
    1 cup HERSHEY₂S Semi-Sweet Chocolate Chips

Preheat oven to 350°F. In large bowl, combine cake mix, oats, butter and eggs; mix well. Stir in chocolate chips. Drop by rounded teaspoonfuls onto ungreased cookie sheets.

Bake 10 to 12 minutes or until very lightly browned. Cool slightly; remove from cookie sheets to wire racks. Cool completely.

Makes about 4 dozen cookies

Cowboy Cookies

½ cup butter or margarine, softened
½ cup packed light brown sugar
¼ cup granulated sugar
1 egg
1 teaspoon vanilla
1 cup all-purpose flour
2 tablespoons unsweetened cocoa powder
½ teaspoon baking powder
¼ teaspoon baking soda
1 cup uncooked rolled oats
1 cup (6 ounces) semisweet chocolate chips
½ cup raisins
½ cup chopped nuts

Preheat oven to 375°F. Lightly grease cookie sheets or line with parchment paper.

Beat butter with sugars in large bowl until blended. Add egg and vanilla; beat until fluffy. Combine flour, cocoa, baking powder and baking soda in small bowl; stir into butter mixture. Add oats, chocolate chips, raisins and nuts. Drop by rounded teaspoonfuls 2 inches apart onto prepared cookie sheets.

Bake 10 to 12 minutes or until lightly browned around edges. Remove to wire racks to cool.

Makes about 4 dozen cookies

Cowboy Cookies

Chocolate Chip Caramel Nut Cookies

18 caramels, unwrapped
1 BUTTER FLAVOR* CRISCO® Stick or 1 cup BUTTER FLAVOR* CRISCO® all-vegetable shortening
1 cup granulated sugar
½ cup firmly packed brown sugar
2 eggs, beaten
2¾ cups all-purpose flour
1 teaspoon baking soda
1 teaspoon salt
1 teaspoon vanilla
½ teaspoon hot water
1 cup semisweet chocolate chips
½ cup coarsely chopped unsalted peanuts

*Butter Flavor Crisco is artificially flavored.

1. Heat oven to 400°F. **Place** sheets of foil on countertop for cooling cookies.

2. Cut each caramel into 4 pieces. **Cut** each piece into 6 pieces.

3. Combine shortening, granulated sugar and brown sugar in large bowl. **Beat** at medium speed of electric mixer until well blended and creamy. **Beat** in eggs.

4. Combine flour, baking soda and salt. **Add** gradually to shortening mixture at low speed of electric mixer. **Mix** until well blended. **Beat** in vanilla and hot water. **Stir** in caramels, chocolate chips and nuts with spoon. **Drop** 2 slightly rounded tablespoonfuls of dough for each cookie, 3 inches apart on ungreased baking sheets. **Shape** dough into circles, 2 inches in diameter and 1 inch high.

5. Bake one baking sheet at a time at 400°F for 7 to 9 minutes or until light golden brown. *Do not overbake.* **Cool** 5 minutes on baking sheets. **Remove** cookies to foil to cool completely. *Makes 2 to 2½ dozen cookies*

Chocolate Scotcheroos

1 cup light corn syrup
1 cup sugar
1 cup peanut butter
6 cups KELLOGG'S® RICE KRISPIES® cereal
1 cup (6-ounce package) semisweet chocolate chips
1 cup (6-ounce package) butterscotch chips

Combine corn syrup and sugar in large saucepan. Cook over medium heat, stirring frequently, until sugar dissolves and mixture begins to boil. Remove from heat; stir in peanut butter. Add Kellogg's® Rice Krispies® cereal. Stir until well coated. Press mixture into 13×9-inch baking pan coated with cooking spray. Set aside.

Melt chocolate and butterscotch chips together in small saucepan over low heat, stirring constantly. Spread evenly over cereal mixture. Let stand until firm. Cut into 2×1-inch bars to serve. *Makes about 4 dozen bars*

Choco-Scutterbotch

⅔ cup BUTTER FLAVOR* CRISCO® all-vegetable
    shortening
½ cup firmly packed brown sugar
 2 eggs
 1 package DUNCAN HINES® Moist Deluxe
    Yellow Cake Mix
 1 cup crispy rice cereal
½ cup milk chocolate chunks
½ cup butterscotch chips
½ cup semisweet chocolate chips
½ cup coarsely chopped walnuts or pecans

*Butter Flavor Crisco is artificially flavored.

1. Preheat oven to 375°F.

2. Combine Butter Flavor Crisco® and brown sugar in large
bowl. Beat at medium speed of electric mixer until well
blended. Beat in eggs.

3. Add cake mix gradually at low speed. Mix until well
blended. Stir in cereal, chocolate chunks, butterscotch chips,
chocolate chips and nuts with spoon. Stir until well blended.
Shape dough into 1¼-inch balls. Place 2 inches apart on
ungreased cookie sheets. Flatten slightly to form circles.

4. Bake at 375°F for 7 to 9 minutes or until lightly browned
around edges. Cool 2 minutes before removing to wire racks.
Makes about 3 dozen cookies

REESE'S® Chewy Chocolate Cookies

1¼ cups butter or margarine, softened
  2 cups sugar
  2 eggs
  2 teaspoons vanilla extract
  2 cups all-purpose flour
¾ cup HERSHEY'S Cocoa
 1 teaspoon baking soda
½ teaspoon salt
1⅔ cups (10-ounce package) REESE'S® Peanut
    Butter Chips
½ cup finely chopped nuts (optional)

Preheat oven to 350°F. In large bowl, beat butter and sugar
until light and fluffy. Add eggs and vanilla; beat well. In
medium bowl, combine flour, cocoa, baking soda and salt;
gradually blend into butter mixture. Stir in peanut butter chips
and nuts, if desired. Drop by rounded teaspoonfuls onto
ungreased cookie sheets.

Bake 8 to 9 minutes. (Do not overbake, cookies will be soft.
They will puff while baking and flatten while cooling). Cool
slightly; remove from cookie sheets to wire racks. Cool
completely. *Makes about 4½ dozen cookies*

Peanut Butter Jumbos

½ cup butter or margarine, softened
1 cup packed brown sugar
1 cup granulated sugar
1½ cups peanut butter
3 eggs
2 teaspoons baking soda
1 teaspoon vanilla
4½ cups uncooked rolled oats
1 cup (6 ounces) semisweet chocolate chips
1 cup candy-coated chocolate pieces

Preheat oven to 350°F. Lightly grease cookie sheets or line with parchment paper.

Beat butter, sugars, peanut butter and eggs in large bowl until well blended. Blend in baking soda, vanilla and oats until well mixed. Stir in chocolate chips and candy pieces.

Scoop out about ⅓ cupful of dough for each cookie. Place on prepared cookie sheets, spacing about 4 inches apart. Press each cookie to flatten slightly. Bake 15 to 20 minutes or until firm in center. Remove to wire racks to cool.

Makes about 1½ dozen cookies

Clockwise from top: Peanut Butter Jumbos and White Chocolate Biggies (page 40)

Quick Peanut Butter Chocolate Chip Cookies

1 package DUNCAN HINES® Moist Deluxe
     Yellow Cake Mix
½ cup JIF® Creamy Peanut Butter
½ cup butter or margarine, softened
2 eggs
1 cup milk chocolate chips

1. Preheat oven to 350°F. Grease cookie sheets.

2. Combine cake mix, peanut butter, butter and eggs in large bowl. Mix at low speed with electric mixer until blended. Stir in chocolate chips.

3. Drop by rounded teaspoonfuls onto prepared cookie sheets. Bake 9 to 11 minutes or until lightly browned. Cool 2 minutes on cookie sheets. Remove to cooling racks.

Makes about 4 dozen cookies

Tip: *You can use JIF® Extra Crunchy Peanut Butter in place of regular peanut butter.*

Peanut Butter Chocolate Chip Cookies

1 cup sugar
½ cup SKIPPY® Creamy or Super Chunk Peanut
     Butter
½ cup evaporated milk
1 (6-ounce) package semisweet chocolate chips
1 cup coarsely chopped nuts

Preheat oven to 325°F.

In medium bowl, mix sugar and peanut butter until well blended. Stir in evaporated milk, chips and nuts until well blended. Drop by rounded teaspoonfuls 2½ inches apart onto foil-lined cookie sheets. Spread batter evenly into 2-inch circles. Bake 18 to 20 minutes or until golden. Cool completely on foil-lined wire racks.   *Makes about 3½ dozen cookies*

Chocolate & Peanut-Butter Tweed Cookies

1 cup butter or margarine, softened
½ cup packed light brown sugar
¼ cup granulated sugar
1 egg
¼ teaspoon baking soda
2½ cups all-purpose flour
½ cup *each* semisweet chocolate chips and
     peanut butter chips, chopped*

*Chips can be chopped in a food processor.

Beat butter and sugars in large bowl with electric mixer until smooth. Add egg and baking soda; beat until light and fluffy. Stir in flour until dough is smooth. Blend in chopped chips. Divide dough into 4 parts. Shape each part into a roll, about 1½ inches in diameter. Wrap in plastic wrap; refrigerate until firm, at least 1 hour or up to 2 weeks. (For longer storage, freeze up to 6 weeks.)

Preheat oven to 375°F. Lightly grease cookie sheets or line with parchment paper. Cut rolls into ⅛-inch-thick slices; place 2 inches apart on prepared cookie sheets. Bake 10 to 12 minutes or until lightly browned. Remove to wire racks to cool completely.   *Makes about 6 dozen cookies*

Tracy's Pizza-Pan Cookies

   1 cup butter or margarine, softened
   ¾ cup granulated sugar
   ¾ cup packed brown sugar
   1 package (8 ounces) cream cheese, softened
   1 teaspoon vanilla
   2 eggs
  2¼ cups all-purpose flour
   1 teaspoon baking soda
   ¼ teaspoon salt
   1 package (12 ounces) semisweet chocolate
      chips
   1 cup chopped walnuts or pecans

Preheat oven to 375°F. Lightly grease 2 (12-inch) pizza pans.

Beat butter, sugars, cream cheese and vanilla in large bowl. Add eggs; beat until well blended. Combine flour, baking soda and salt in small bowl. Add to butter mixture; blend well. Stir in chocolate chips and nuts. Divide dough in half; press each half evenly into a prepared pan.

Bake 20 to 25 minutes or until lightly browned around edges. Cool completely in pans on wire racks. To serve, cut into slim wedges or break into pieces.   *Makes 2 (12-inch) cookies*

White Chocolate Biggies

  1½ cups butter or margarine, softened
   1 cup granulated sugar
   ¾ cup packed light brown sugar
   2 teaspoons vanilla
   2 eggs
  2½ cups all-purpose flour
   ⅔ cup unsweetened cocoa powder
   1 teaspoon baking soda
   ½ teaspoon salt
   1 package (10 ounces) large white chocolate
      chips *or* 1 white chocolate bar, cut into
      pieces
   ¾ cup pecan halves, coarsely chopped
   ½ cup golden raisins

Preheat oven to 350°F. Lightly grease cookie sheets or line with parchment paper.

Beat butter, sugars, vanilla and eggs in large bowl until light and fluffy. Combine flour, cocoa, baking soda and salt in medium bowl; blend into butter mixture until smooth. Stir in white chocolate chips, pecans and raisins.

Scoop out about ⅓ cupful of dough for each cookie. Place on prepared cookie sheets, spacing about 4 inches apart. Press each cookie to flatten slightly.

Bake 12 to 14 minutes or until firm in center. Cool 5 minutes on cookie sheets, then remove to wire racks to cool completely.
Makes about 2 dozen cookies

Jumbo Chunky Cookies

1 cup (2 sticks) margarine or butter, softened
¾ cup packed brown sugar
¾ cup granulated sugar
2 eggs
1 teaspoon vanilla
1¾ cups all-purpose flour
½ cup quick oats
1 teaspoon baking soda
½ teaspoon cinnamon
¼ teaspoon salt
1 (8-ounce) package BAKER'S® Semi-Sweet
    Chocolate, cut into chunks, *or*
    1 (12-ounce) package BAKER'S®
    Semi-Sweet Real Chocolate Chips
1 cup BAKER'S® ANGEL FLAKE® Coconut
⅔ cup chopped nuts
½ cup raisins (optional)

Heat oven to 375°F.

Beat margarine, sugars, eggs and vanilla until light and fluffy. Mix in flour, oats, baking soda, cinnamon and salt.

Stir in chocolate, coconut, nuts and raisins, if desired. Drop by rounded tablespoonfuls, 2½ inches apart, onto ungreased cookie sheets.

Bake for 15 minutes or until golden brown. Remove from cookie sheets to cool on wire racks.

Makes about 2½ dozen cookies

Prep Time: 20 minutes
Bake Time: 15 minutes

Jumbo Chunky Cookies

Island Cookies

1⅔ cups all-purpose flour
¾ teaspoon baking powder
½ teaspoon baking soda
½ teaspoon salt
¾ cup (1½ sticks) butter or margarine, softened
¾ cup packed brown sugar
⅓ cup granulated sugar
1 teaspoon vanilla extract
1 egg
2 cups (11½-ounce package) NESTLÉ® Toll House® Milk Chocolate Morsels
1 cup flaked coconut, toasted if desired
¾ cup macadamia nuts or walnuts, chopped

Combine flour, baking powder, baking soda and salt in small bowl.

Beat butter, brown sugar, granulated sugar and vanilla in large bowl until creamy. Beat in egg. Gradually blend in flour mixture. Stir in morsels, coconut and nuts. Drop by slightly rounded tablespoon onto ungreased baking sheets.

Bake in preheated 375°F oven for 8 to 11 minutes or until edges are lightly browned. Let stand for 2 minutes. Remove from cookie sheets; cool on wire racks.

Makes about 2 dozen cookies

Note: *NESTLÉ® Toll House® Semi-Sweet Chocolate Morsels, Semi-Sweet Chocolate Mini Morsels, Mint-Chocolate Morsels, Premier White Morsels or Butterscotch Morsels may be substituted for the Milk Chocolate Morsels.*

"M & M's®" Chocolate Candies Easy Party Cookies

2¼ cups all-purpose flour
1 teaspoon salt
1 teaspoon baking soda
1 cup butter or margarine, softened
1 cup packed light brown sugar
½ cup granulated sugar
2 eggs
2 teaspoons vanilla
1½ cups "M & M's®" Plain Chocolate Candies, divided

Preheat oven to 375°F. In medium bowl, combine flour, salt and baking soda. Set aside.

In large bowl, beat butter, brown sugar and granulated sugar until light and fluffy. Blend in eggs and vanilla. Gradually beat in flour mixture; mix well. Stir in ½ cup candies. Drop by rounded teaspoonfuls onto ungreased cookie sheets. Press 2 or 3 additional candies into each cookie.

Bake 10 to 12 minutes or until golden brown. Cool completely on wire racks.

Makes about 6 dozen cookies

Best-Ever Bars

Apricot Crumb Squares

1 package (18.25 ounces) light yellow cake mix
1 teaspoon ground cinnamon
½ teaspoon ground nutmeg
6 tablespoons cold margarine, cut into pieces
¾ cup uncooked multigrain oatmeal cereal or rolled oats
1 whole egg
2 egg whites
1 tablespoon water
1 jar (10 ounces) apricot fruit spread
2 tablespoons firmly packed light brown sugar

Preheat oven to 350°F. Combine cake mix, cinnamon and nutmeg in medium bowl. Cut in margarine with pastry blender or 2 knives until coarse crumbs form. Stir in cereal. Reserve 1 cup mixture. Mix egg, egg whites and water into remaining mixture.

Spread batter evenly in ungreased 13×9-inch baking pan; top with fruit spread. Sprinkle reserved 1 cup cereal mixture over fruit; top with brown sugar.

Bake 35 to 40 minutes or until top is golden brown. Cool in pan on wire rack; cut into squares.

Makes about 15 squares

Apricot Meringue Squares

1 cup butter, softened
⅓ cup granulated sugar
1 teaspoon vanilla
2 teaspoons grated orange peel
2 cups all-purpose flour
1 jar (12 ounces) apricot jam
2 tablespoons orange juice
2 egg whites
1 cup powdered sugar
   Slivered almonds (optional)

Preheat oven to 350°F. Beat butter, granulated sugar, vanilla and orange peel in large bowl with electric mixer at medium speed until light and fluffy. Gradually add flour, beating at low speed until smooth.

Press dough into ungreased 13×9-inch baking pan. Bake 15 minutes. Cool completely on wire rack. *Do not turn oven off.*

Combine jam and orange juice in small bowl; beat until smooth. Spread over cooled crust.

Beat egg whites in clean large bowl with electric mixer at high speed until foamy. Gradually beat in powdered sugar until stiff peaks form. Spread meringue over jam mixture with rubber spatula.

Bake 15 to 20 minutes or until light golden brown. Cool completely on wire rack. Cut into 2-inch squares. Garnish with almonds, if desired. *Makes about 24 squares*

Tropical Sun Bars

CRUST
1 cup all-purpose flour
¼ cup sugar
⅓ cup margarine, softened
1 tablespoon grated tangerine or orange peel
FILLING
½ cup sugar
½ cup flaked coconut
2 tablespoons all-purpose flour
½ teaspoon baking powder
⅛ teaspoon salt
1½ tablespoons grated tangerine or orange peel
2 eggs
1 tablespoon orange juice
1 tablespoon orange liqueur
   Thin strips of orange peel (optional)

Preheat oven to 350°F. For crust, combine 1 cup flour, ¼ cup sugar, margarine and 1 tablespoon tangerine peel in small mixer bowl. Beat at low speed of electric mixer, scraping bowl often, until coarse crumbs form, 1 to 2 minutes. Press on bottom of 9-inch square baking pan. Bake 10 to 12 minutes or until edges are lightly browned.

For filling, combine ½ cup sugar, coconut, 2 tablespoons flour, baking powder, salt, 1½ tablespoons tangerine peel, eggs, orange juice and liqueur in small mixer bowl. Beat at medium speed, scraping bowl often, until well blended, 1 to 2 minutes. Pour over hot crust. Bake 20 to 25 minutes or until edges are lightly browned. Immediately sprinkle with orange peel, if desired. Cool completely. Cut into bars.

Makes about 24 bars

California Apricot Power Bars

2 cups (12 ounces) California dried apricot halves, coarsely chopped

1¼ cups (8 ounces) pitted dates, coarsely chopped

2½ cups (10 ounces) pecans, coarsely chopped

1¼ cups whole wheat flour

1 teaspoon baking powder

3 eggs

1 cup packed brown sugar

¼ cup apple juice or water

1½ teaspoons vanilla

Preheat oven to 350°F. Line 15½×10½×1-inch jelly roll pan with foil. In large bowl, stir together apricots, dates and pecans; divide in half. Combine flour and baking powder; add to half of fruit mixture. Toss to coat. In medium bowl, combine eggs, sugar, apple juice and vanilla; stir into flour mixture until thoroughly moistened. Spread batter evenly into prepared pan. Press remaining fruit mixture lightly on top.

Bake 20 minutes or until golden and bars spring back when pressed lightly. Cool in pan 5 minutes. Turn out onto wire rack; cool 45 minutes. Peel off foil and cut into bars. Store in airtight container.   *Makes about 32 bars*

Favorite recipe from **California Apricot Advisory Board**

California Apricot Power Bars

Cherry Butterscotch Bars

2 cups plus 1 tablespoon all-purpose flour, divided
¾ cup packed brown sugar
¾ cup margarine, softened
2 eggs
¼ cup butterscotch chips, melted
1 teaspoon baking powder
¼ teaspoon salt
1 teaspoon vanilla
¾ cup chopped maraschino cherries, drained, divided
¾ cup butterscotch chips, divided
Powdered sugar (optional)

Preheat oven to 350°F. Grease and flour 13×9-inch baking pan. Set aside.

Combine 2 cups flour, brown sugar, margarine, eggs, melted chips, baking powder, salt and vanilla in large mixer bowl. Beat at low speed of electric mixer, scraping bowl often, until well blended, 1 to 2 minutes. Mix ½ cup chopped cherries and remaining 1 tablespoon flour in small bowl; add to margarine mixture. Blend ½ cup butterscotch chips into margarine mixture. Pour into prepared baking pan.

Bake 25 to 35 minutes or until edges are lightly browned. Cool completely. Top with remaining ¼ cup cherries and ¼ cup chips. Sprinkle with powdered sugar, if desired. Cut into bars.

Makes about 36 bars

Pear Blondies

1 cup packed brown sugar
¼ cup butter or margarine, melted
1 egg
½ teaspoon vanilla
¾ cup all-purpose flour
½ teaspoon baking powder
½ teaspoon salt
1 cup chopped firm-ripe fresh U.S.A. Anjou, Bosc, Bartlett, Nelis or Seckel pears
⅓ cup semisweet chocolate chips

Preheat oven to 350°F. Grease 8-inch square baking pan. Set aside.

Combine brown sugar, butter, egg and vanilla in medium bowl; blend well. Combine flour, baking powder and salt in small bowl; stir into brown sugar mixture. Stir in pears and chips. Spread in prepared baking pan. Bake 30 to 35 minutes or until golden brown. Cool completely in pan on wire rack. Cut into 2-inch squares.

Makes 16 squares

Favorite recipe from **Oregon Washington California Pear Bureau**

Peachy Oatmeal Bars

CRUMB MIXTURE
1½ cups all-purpose flour
1 cup uncooked rolled oats
½ cup sugar
¾ cup margarine, melted
½ teaspoon baking soda
¼ teaspoon salt
2 teaspoons almond extract
FILLING
¾ cup peach preserves
⅓ cup flaked coconut

Preheat oven to 350°F. Grease 9-inch square baking pan. Set aside.

For crumb mixture, combine flour, oats, sugar, margarine, baking soda, salt and almond extract in large mixer bowl. Beat at low speed of electric mixer, scraping bowl often, until mixture is crumbly, 1 to 2 minutes. Reserve ¾ cup crumb mixture; press remaining crumb mixture onto bottom of prepared baking pan.

For filling, spread peach preserves to within ½ inch of edge of crumb mixture; sprinkle reserved crumb mixture and coconut over top. Bake 22 to 27 minutes or until edges are lightly browned. Cool completely. Cut into bars.

Makes 24 to 30 bars

Strawberry Streusel Bars

CRUMB MIXTURE
2 cups all-purpose flour
1 cup sugar
¾ cup pecans, coarsely chopped
1 cup butter or margarine, softened
1 egg
FILLING
1 jar (10 ounces) strawberry preserves

Preheat oven to 350°F. Grease 9-inch square baking pan. Set aside.

For crumb mixture, combine flour, sugar, pecans, butter and egg in large mixer bowl. Beat at low speed of electric mixer, scraping bowl often, until mixture is crumbly, 2 to 3 minutes. Reserve 1 cup crumb mixture; press remaining crumb mixture onto bottom of prepared baking pan. Spread preserves to within ½ inch of edge of unbaked crumb mixture. Crumble remaining crumb mixture over preserves. Bake 42 to 50 minutes or until lightly browned. Cool completely. Cut into bars.

Makes about 24 bars

Top to bottom: Peachy Oatmeal Bars and Strawberry Streusel Bars

Layered Lemon Crumb Bars

1 (14-ounce) can EAGLE® Brand Sweetened
  Condensed Milk (NOT evaporated milk)
½ cup REALEMON® Lemon Juice from
  Concentrate
1 teaspoon grated lemon peel
⅔ cup margarine or butter, softened
1 cup firmly packed light brown sugar
1½ cups flour
1 cup quick-cooking oats, uncooked
1 teaspoon baking powder
½ teaspoon salt
½ teaspoon ground cinnamon
½ teaspoon ground nutmeg

Preheat oven to 350°F (325°F for glass dish). In small bowl, combine sweetened condensed milk, REALEMON® brand and peel; set aside. In large bowl, beat margarine and brown sugar until fluffy; add flour, oats, baking powder and salt. Mix until crumbly. Press half the oat mixture on bottom of lightly greased 13×9-inch baking pan. Top with lemon mixture. Stir spices into remaining crumb mixture; sprinkle evenly over lemon layer.

Bake 20 to 25 minutes or until lightly browned. Cool. Chill. Cut into bars. Store covered in refrigerator.

Makes 24 to 36 bars

*Top to bottom: Double Peanut-Choco Bars (page 72),
Chocolate Mint Bars (page 68) and
Layered Lemon Crumb Bars*

Banana Gingerbread Bars

1 extra-ripe, medium DOLE® Banana, peeled
1 package (14.5 ounce) gingerbread cake mix
½ cup lukewarm water
1 egg
1 small DOLE® Banana, peeled and chopped
½ cup DOLE® Raisins
½ cup DOLE® Slivered Almonds
1½ cups powdered sugar
   Juice from 1 DOLE® Lemon

• Preheat oven to 350°F.

• Purée medium banana in blender to measure ½ cup.

• In large mixer bowl, combine gingerbread mix, water, banana purée and egg. Beat on low speed of electric mixer 1 minute.

• Stir in chopped banana (½ cup), raisins and almonds.

• Spread batter in greased 13×9-inch baking pan. Bake 20 to 25 minutes or until top springs back when lightly touched.

• In medium bowl, mix powdered sugar and 3 tablespoons lemon juice to make thin glaze. Spread over warm gingerbread. Cool before cutting into bars. Sprinkle with additional powdered sugar, if desired.

Makes about 32 bars

Banana Split Bars

⅓ cup margarine or butter, softened
1 cup sugar
1 egg
1 banana, mashed
½ teaspoon vanilla
1¼ cups all-purpose flour
1 teaspoon CALUMET® Baking Powder
¼ teaspoon salt
⅓ cup chopped nuts
2 cups KRAFT® Miniature Marshmallows
1 cup BAKER'S® Semi-Sweet Real Chocolate Chips
⅓ cup maraschino cherries, drained and quartered

Heat oven to 350°F.

Beat margarine and sugar until light and fluffy. Add egg, banana and vanilla; mix well. Mix in flour, baking powder and salt. Stir in nuts. Pour batter into greased 13×9-inch pan.

Bake for 20 minutes. Remove from oven. Sprinkle with marshmallows, chips and cherries. Bake 10 to 15 minutes longer or until wooden pick inserted in center comes out clean. Cool in pan; cut into bars. *Makes about 24 bars*

Prep time: 25 minutes
Bake time: 30 to 35 minutes

Kahlúa® Pumpkin Squares with Praline Topping

> 1 cup all-purpose flour
> ¼ cup powdered sugar
> ½ cup cold unsalted butter
> 1 cup LIBBY'S® Solid Pack Pumpkin
> 1 (8-ounce) package cream cheese, cut up and softened
> 2 eggs
> ¼ cup granulated sugar
> ¼ cup KAHLÚA®
> 1 cup chopped walnuts or pecans
> ¾ cup firmly packed brown sugar
> ¼ cup unsalted butter, melted

Preheat oven to 350°F. In medium bowl, combine flour and powdered sugar. Using 2 knives or pastry blender, cut in ½ cup butter until mixture forms fine crumbs. Press mixture into bottom of 8-inch square baking dish. Bake 15 to 18 minutes or until golden.

Meanwhile, in food processor or blender, purée pumpkin, cream cheese, eggs, granulated sugar and Kahlúa® until smooth. Pour pumpkin mixture over warm baked crust; return to oven and bake about 20 minutes or until set. Cool in dish on wire rack. Cover; refrigerate.

In small bowl, combine nuts, brown sugar and melted butter. Just before serving, sprinkle nut mixture over pumpkin filling.

Makes about 16 squares

Raspberry Coconut Layer Bars

> 1⅔ cups graham cracker crumbs
> ½ cup butter, melted
> 2⅔ cups (7-ounce package) flaked coconut
> 1¼ cups (14-ounce can) CARNATION®
>   Sweetened Condensed Milk
> 1 cup red raspberry jam or preserves
> ⅓ cup finely chopped walnuts, toasted
> ½ cup semisweet chocolate pieces, melted
> ¼ cup vanilla milk chocolate pieces, melted

Preheat oven to 350°F. In medium bowl, combine graham cracker crumbs and butter. Spread evenly over bottom of 13×9-inch baking pan, pressing firmly to make crust. Sprinkle coconut over crust. Pour sweetened condensed milk evenly over coconut. Bake 20 to 25 minutes or until lightly browned. Cool. Spread jam over coconut layer. Chill 3 to 4 hours. Sprinkle with walnuts. Drizzle melted chocolates over top layer, creating lacy effect. Chill. Cut into 3×1½-inch bars.

Makes about 24 bars

Top to bottom: Raspberry Coconut Layer Bars and Kahlúa® Pumpkin Squares with Praline Topping

Pumpkin Cheesecake Bars

Pumpkin Cheesecake Bars

  1 cup all-purpose flour
  ⅓ cup packed light brown sugar
  5 tablespoons cold butter or margarine
  ½ cup pecans, finely chopped
  1 (8-ounce) package cream cheese, softened
  ¾ cup granulated sugar
  ½ cup LIBBY'S® Solid Pack Pumpkin
  2 eggs, lightly beaten
1½ teaspoons ground cinnamon
  1 teaspoon ground allspice
  1 teaspoon vanilla extract
  Glazed Pecan Halves (recipe follows)

Preheat oven to 350°F. In medium bowl, combine flour and brown sugar. Cut in butter to make crumb mixture. Stir in nuts. Reserve ¾ cup mixture for topping. Press remaining mixture into bottom of 8-inch square baking pan. Bake 15 minutes. Cool slightly.

In large bowl, combine cream cheese, granulated sugar, pumpkin, eggs, cinnamon, allspice, and vanilla; blend until smooth. Pour over baked crust. Sprinkle with reserved topping. Bake an additional 35 to 40 minutes or until slightly firm. Cool on wire rack. Cut into 2×1-inch bars and then into triangles, if desired. Garnish each bar with a Glazed Pecan Half.

Makes 32 bars or 64 triangles

Glazed Pecan Halves: Place greased wire rack over cookie sheet. In small saucepan, bring ¼ cup dark corn syrup to a boil. Boil 1 minute, stirring constantly, until syrup slightly thickens. Remove from heat. Add 32 pecan halves, stirring until well coated. With slotted spoon, remove pecans from syrup. Transfer to wire rack; cool. Makes 32 pecan halves.

Blueberry Cheesecake Bars

    1 package DUNCAN HINES® Bakery Style
        Blueberry Muffin Mix
    ¼ cup cold butter or margarine
    ⅓ cup finely chopped pecans
    1 (8-ounce) package cream cheese, softened
    ½ cup sugar
    1 egg
    3 tablespoons lemon juice
    1 teaspoon grated lemon peel

1. Preheat oven to 350°F. Grease 9-inch square pan.

2. Rinse blueberries from Mix with cold water and drain.

3. Place muffin mix in medium bowl; cut in butter with pastry blender or two knives. Stir in pecans. Press into bottom of prepared pan. Bake 15 minutes or until set.

4. Combine cream cheese and sugar in medium bowl. Beat until smooth. Add egg, lemon juice and lemon peel. Beat well. Spread over baked crust. Sprinkle with blueberries. Sprinkle topping packet from Mix over blueberries. Return to oven. Bake 35 to 40 minutes or until filling is set. Cool completely. Refrigerate until ready to serve. Cut into bars.

Makes about 16 bars

Blueberry Cheesecake Bars

Toffee-Bran Bars

¾ cup all-purpose flour
¾ cup **NABISCO®** 100% Bran, divided
1¼ cups firmly packed light brown sugar,
    divided
½ cup margarine, melted
2 eggs, slightly beaten
1 teaspoon **DAVIS®** Baking Powder
1 teaspoon vanilla extract
1 cup semisweet chocolate chips
½ cup flaked coconut, toasted
⅓ cup chopped walnuts

Preheat oven to 350°F. In small bowl, combine flour, ½ cup bran, ½ cup brown sugar and margarine. Press on bottom of 13×9×2-inch baking pan. Bake 10 minutes; set aside.

In medium bowl, with electric mixer at high speed, beat remaining ¼ cup bran, ¾ cup brown sugar, eggs, baking powder and vanilla until thick and foamy. Spread over prepared crust. Bake 25 minutes more or until set. Remove pan from oven. Sprinkle with chocolate chips; let stand 5 minutes. Spread softened chocolate evenly over baked layer. Immediately sprinkle coconut and chopped walnuts in alternating diagonal strips over chocolate. Cool completely in pan on wire rack. Cut into 3×1½-inch bars. Store in airtight container. *Makes 24 bars*

Toffee Bars

½ cup margarine or butter, melted
1 cup quick-cooking oats, uncooked
½ cup firmly packed brown sugar
½ cup flour
½ cup finely chopped walnuts
¼ teaspoon baking soda
1 (14-ounce) can **EAGLE®** Brand Sweetened
    Condensed Milk (NOT evaporated milk)
2 teaspoons vanilla extract
1 (6-ounce) package semisweet chocolate
    chips (1 cup)

Preheat oven to 350°F. In medium bowl, combine *6 tablespoons* margarine, oats, brown sugar, flour, nuts and baking soda. Press firmly on bottom of greased 13×9-inch baking pan; bake 10 to 15 minutes or until lightly browned.

In medium saucepan, over medium heat, cook and stir remaining *2 tablespoons* margarine and sweetened condensed milk until mixture thickens slightly, about 15 minutes. Remove from heat; stir in vanilla. Pour over crust. Return to oven; bake 10 to 15 minutes longer or until golden brown. Remove from oven; *immediately* sprinkle with chips. Let stand 1 minute; spread while still warm. Cool. Cut into bars. Store tightly covered at room temperature. *Makes 24 to 36 bars*

*Clockwise from top: Toffee-Bran Bars
and Chewy Bar Cookies (page 74)*

Caramel Marshmallow Bars

CRUMB MIXTURE
  1¼ cups all-purpose flour
  ¼ cup graham cracker crumbs
  ½ cup sugar
  ½ cup butter or margarine, softened
  ¼ teaspoon salt
  ½ cup chopped salted peanuts
FILLING
  ¾ cup caramel ice cream topping
  ½ cup salted peanuts
  ½ cups miniature marshmallows
  ½ cup milk chocolate chips

Preheat oven to 350°F. For crumb mixture, combine flour, graham cracker crumbs, sugar, butter and salt in small mixer bowl. Beat at low speed of electric mixer, scraping bowl often, until mixture is crumbly, 1 to 2 minutes. Stir in nuts. Reserve ¾ cup crumb mixture. Press remaining crumb mixture on bottom of greased and floured 9-inch square baking pan. Bake 10 to 12 minutes or until lightly browned.

For filling, spread caramel topping evenly over hot crust. Sprinkle with nuts, marshmallows and chocolate chips. Crumble ¾ cup reserved crumb mixture over chocolate chips. Continue baking 10 to 12 minutes or until marshmallows just start to brown. Cool on wire rack about 30 minutes. Cover; refrigerate 1 to 2 hours or until firm. Cut into bars.

Makes about 30 bars

Caramel Marshmallow Bars

Caramel Apple Oat Squares

1¾ cups flour
1 cup quick-cooking oats
½ cup firmly packed brown sugar
½ teaspoon baking soda
½ teaspoon salt
1 cup cold margarine or butter
1 cup chopped walnuts
20 caramels, unwrapped
1 (14-ounce) can EAGLE® Brand Sweetened Condensed Milk (NOT evaporated milk)
1 (21-ounce) can COMSTOCK® Brand Apple Filling or Topping

Preheat oven to 375°F. In large bowl, combine flour, oats, sugar, baking soda and salt; cut in margarine until crumbly. Reserving 1½ cups crumb mixture, press remainder on bottom of 13×9-inch baking pan. Bake 15 minutes.

Add walnuts to reserved crumb mixture. Set aside. In medium, heavy saucepan over low heat, melt caramels with sweetened condensed milk, stirring until smooth.

Spoon apple filling into warm crust; top with caramel mixture. Sprinkle with reserved crumb mixture. Bake 20 minutes or until set. Cool. Serve warm with ice cream.

Makes 10 to 12 squares

Caramel Apple Oat Squares

Double Chocolate Crispy Bars

6 cups crispy rice cereal
½ cup peanut butter
⅓ cup butter or margarine
2 squares (1 ounce each) unsweetened
    chocolate
1 package (8 ounces) marshmallows
1 cup (6 ounces) semisweet chocolate chips *or*
    6 ounces bittersweet chocolate, chopped
2 teaspoons shortening, divided
6 ounces white chocolate, chopped

Preheat oven to 350°F. Line 13×9-inch cookie sheet with waxed paper. Spread cereal on cookie sheet; toast in oven 10 minutes or until crispy. Place in large bowl.

Meanwhile, combine peanut butter, butter and unsweetened chocolate in large, heavy saucepan. Stir over low heat until chocolate is melted. Add marshmallows; stir until melted and smooth. Pour peanut butter mixture over cereal; mix until evenly coated. Press into prepared pan.

Place semisweet chocolate and 1 teaspoon shortening in medium bowl. Place bowl over very warm water; stir until chocolate is melted. Spread top of bars with melted chocolate; cool until chocolate is set. Turn bars out of pan onto sheet of waxed paper, chocolate side down. Remove waxed paper from bottom of bars. Melt white chocolate and remaining 1 teaspoon shortening following semisweet chocolate directions above. Spread melted white chocolate over bottoms of bars. Cool until white chocolate is set. Cut into 2×1½-inch bars using sharp, thin knife. *Makes 36 bars*

Chocolate Macadamia Bars

12 squares (1 ounce each) bittersweet chocolate
    or **1 package (12 ounces) semisweet**
    chocolate chips
1 package (8 ounces) cream cheese, softened
⅔ cup whipping cream or undiluted evaporated
    milk
1 cup chopped macadamia nuts or almonds
1 teaspoon vanilla, divided
1 cup butter or margarine, softened
1½ cups sugar
1 egg
3 cups all-purpose flour
1 teaspoon baking powder
¼ teaspoon salt

Preheat oven to 375°F. Lightly grease 13×9-inch baking pan.

Combine chocolate, cream cheese and whipping cream in large, heavy saucepan. Stir over low heat until chocolate is melted and mixture is smooth. Remove from heat; stir in nuts and ½ teaspoon vanilla. Set aside.

Beat butter and sugar in large bowl. Beat in egg and remaining ½ teaspoon vanilla. Add flour, baking powder and salt; blend well. Press half of butter mixture on bottom of prepared pan. Spread chocolate mixture evenly over top. Sprinkle remaining butter mixture over chocolate mixture.

Bake 35 to 40 minutes or until golden brown. Cool in pan on wire rack. Cut into 2×1½-inch bars. *Makes 36 bars*

Counterclockwise from top left: Double Chocolate Crispy Bars, Chocolate Macadamia Bars and Naomi's Revel Bars (page 64)

Naomi's Revel Bars

1 cup plus 2 tablespoons butter or margarine, softened, divided
2 cups packed brown sugar
2 eggs
2 teaspoons vanilla
2½ cups all-purpose flour
1 teaspoon baking soda
3 cups rolled oats, uncooked
1 package (12 ounces) semisweet chocolate chips
1 can (14 ounces) sweetened condensed milk

Preheat oven to 325°F. Lightly grease 13×9-inch baking pan.

Beat 1 cup butter and brown sugar in large bowl. Add eggs; beat until light and fluffy. Blend in vanilla. Combine flour and baking soda in medium bowl; stir into butter mixture. Blend in oats. Spread ¾ oat mixture in prepared pan.

Combine chocolate chips, sweetened condensed milk and remaining 2 tablespoons butter in small, heavy saucepan. Stir over low heat until chocolate is melted. Pour chocolate mixture evenly over oat mixture in pan. Dot with remaining oat mixture.

Bake 20 to 25 minutes or until edges are browned and center feels firm. Cool in pan on wire rack. Cut into 2×1½-inch bars.
Makes 36 bars

Choco Cheesecake Squares

⅓ cup butter or margarine, softened
⅓ cup packed light brown sugar
1 cup plus 1 tablespoon all-purpose flour, divided
½ cup chopped pecans (optional)
1 cup semisweet chocolate chips
1 package (8 ounces) cream cheese, softened
¼ cup granulated sugar
1 egg
1 teaspoon vanilla

Preheat oven to 350°F. Grease 8-inch square baking pan; set aside. Beat butter and brown sugar in large bowl until light and fluffy. Add 1 cup flour. Beat until well combined. Stir in nuts, if desired. (Mixture will be crumbly.) Press evenly into prepared pan. Bake 15 minutes.

Place chocolate chips in 1-cup glass measuring cup. Melt in microwave oven at HIGH 2½ to 3 minutes, stirring after 2 minutes. Beat cream cheese and granulated sugar in medium bowl until light and fluffy. Add remaining 1 tablespoon flour, egg and vanilla; beat until smooth. Gradually stir in melted chocolate, mixing well. Pour cream cheese mixture over partially baked crust. Return to oven; bake 15 minutes or until set. Remove pan to wire rack; cool completely. Cut into 2-inch squares.
Makes about 16 squares

Choco Cheesecake Squares

Chocolate-Drizzled Peanut Bars

Bar Cookie Crust (page 67)
½ cup packed brown sugar
⅓ cup KARO® Light Corn Syrup
¼ cup MAZOLA® Margarine
¼ cup heavy cream
1 teaspoon vanilla
¼ teaspoon lemon juice
1½ cups coarsely chopped roasted peanuts
Chocolate Glaze (recipe follows)

Preheat oven to 350°F. Prepare Bar Cookie Crust according to recipe directions. In medium saucepan, combine brown sugar, corn syrup, margarine and cream. Bring to a boil over medium heat; remove from heat. Stir in vanilla, lemon juice and peanuts. Pour over hot crust; spread evenly. Bake 15 to 20 minutes or until set. Cool completely on wire rack. Drizzle with Chocolate Glaze; cool before cutting into bars.

Makes about 60 bars

Prep Time: 30 minutes
Bake Time: 20 minutes, plus cooling

Chocolate Glaze: In small, heavy saucepan, over low heat, combine ⅔ cup semisweet chocolate chips and 1 tablespoon MAZOLA® Margarine; stir until melted and smooth.

Clockwise from top: Almond Toffee Triangles (page 74), Chocolate-Drizzled Peanut Bars and Chocolate Pecan Pie Squares

Bar Cookie Crust

    MAZOLA® No Stick® cooking spray
2½ cups flour
  1 cup cold MAZOLA® Margarine, cut in pieces
  ½ cup confectioners sugar
  ¼ teaspoon salt

Preheat oven to 350°F. Spray 15×10-inch baking pan with cooking spray. In large bowl, with electric mixer at medium speed, beat flour, margarine, sugar and salt until mixture resembles coarse crumbs; press firmly and evenly into prepared pan. Bake 20 minutes or until golden brown. Top with desired filling. Finish baking according to individual recipe directions.

Chocolate Pecan Pie Squares

    Bar Cookie Crust (recipe above)
1½ cups KARO® Light or Dark Corn Syrup
  1 cup (6 ounces) semisweet chocolate chips
  1 cup sugar
  4 eggs, slightly beaten
1½ teaspoons vanilla
2½ cups coarsely chopped pecans

Preheat oven to 350°F. Prepare Bar Cookie Crust according to recipe directions. In large, heavy saucepan, combine corn syrup and chocolate chips. Stir over low heat just until chocolate melts. Remove from heat. Beat in sugar, eggs and vanilla until blended. Stir in pecans. Pour over hot crust; spread evenly. Bake 30 minutes or until filling is firm around edges and slightly firm in center. Cool completely on wire rack before cutting. *Makes about 24 squares*

Fudgey Almond Bars

  ¾ cup plus ⅓ cup margarine or butter, softened
  ¾ cup confectioners' sugar
1½ cups unsifted flour
  ½ cup HERSHEY'S Cocoa
  1 (14-ounce) can EAGLE® Brand Sweetened Condensed Milk (NOT evaporated milk)
1¼ cups almonds, toasted and coarsely chopped
  ½ cup hot water
  2 eggs, well beaten
  ½ teaspoon almond extract
  ⅛ teaspoon salt

Preheat oven to 350°F. In large bowl, beat *¾ cup* margarine and sugar until well blended. Add flour; mix well. Press on bottom of ungreased 13×9-inch baking pan. Bake 15 minutes or until lightly browned.

Meanwhile, in medium saucepan, over low heat, melt remaining *⅓ cup* margarine; stir in cocoa. Remove from heat; stir in remaining ingredients. Pour evenly over baked crust.

Bake 25 to 30 minutes or until center is set. Cool. Chill thoroughly. Cut into bars. Store covered in refrigerator.
Makes 24 to 36 bars

"Cordially Yours" Chocolate Chip Bars

¾ BUTTER FLAVOR* CRISCO® Stick or ¾ cup BUTTER FLAVOR* CRISCO® all-vegetable shortening
2 eggs
½ cup granulated sugar
¼ cup firmly packed brown sugar
1½ teaspoons vanilla
1 teaspoon almond extract
2 cups all-purpose flour
1 teaspoon baking soda
½ teaspoon cinnamon
1 can (21 ounces) cherry pie filling
1½ cups milk chocolate big chips
Powdered sugar

*Butter Flavor Crisco is artificially flavored.

1. Heat oven to 350°F. **Grease** 15½×10½×1-inch pan with shortening. **Place** cooling rack on countertop.

2. Combine shortening, eggs, granulated sugar, brown sugar, vanilla and almond extract in large bowl. **Beat** at medium speed of electric mixer until well blended.

3. Combine flour, baking soda and cinnamon. **Mix** into shortening mixture at low speed until just blended. **Stir** in pie filling and chocolate chips. **Spread** in prepared pan.

4. Bake at 350°F for 25 minutes or until lightly browned and top springs back when lightly pressed. *Do not overbake.* **Cool** completely on cooling rack. **Sprinkle** with powdered sugar. **Cut** into 2½×2-inch bars. *Makes 30 bars*

Chocolate Mint Bars

1 (6-ounce) package semisweet chocolate chips (1 cup)
1 (14-ounce) can EAGLE® Brand Sweetened Condensed Milk (NOT evaporated milk)
¾ cup plus 2 tablespoons margarine or butter
½ teaspoon peppermint extract
1¼ cups firmly packed light brown sugar
1 egg
1½ cups unsifted flour
1½ cups quick-cooking oats, uncooked
¾ cup chopped nuts
⅓ cup crushed hard peppermint candy, optional

Preheat oven to 350°F. In heavy saucepan, over low heat, melt chips with sweetened condensed milk and *2 tablespoons* margarine; remove from heat. Add extract; set aside.

In large bowl, beat remaining *¾ cup* margarine and brown sugar until fluffy; beat in egg. Add flour and oats; mix well. With floured hands, press two-thirds oat mixture on bottom of greased 15×10-inch baking pan; spread evenly with chocolate mixture. Add nuts to remaining oat mixture; crumble evenly over chocolate. Sprinkle with peppermint candy if desired.

Bake 15 to 18 minutes or until edges are lightly browned. Cool. Cut into bars. Store loosely covered at room temperature. *Makes 36 to 48 bars*

Top to bottom: "Cordially Yours" Chocolate Chip Bars and Peanut Butter Bars (page 81)

Chocolate Caramel-Pecan Bars

2 cups butter, softened, divided
½ cup granulated sugar
1 egg
2¾ cups all-purpose flour
⅔ cup packed light brown sugar
¼ cup light corn syrup
2½ cups coarsely chopped pecans
1 cup semisweet chocolate chips

Preheat oven to 375°F. Grease 15×10-inch jelly-roll pan; set aside. Beat 1 cup butter and granulated sugar in large bowl until light and fluffy. Beat in egg. Add flour. Beat until well combined. Spread dough with rubber spatula into prepared pan. Bake 20 minutes or until light golden brown.

Meanwhile, prepare topping. Combine remaining 1 cup butter, brown sugar and corn syrup in medium, heavy saucepan. Cook over medium heat until mixture boils, stirring frequently. Boil gently 2 minutes, without stirring. Quickly stir in pecans; spread evenly over hot base. Return to oven and bake 20 minutes or until dark golden brown and bubbling. Immediately sprinkle chocolate chips evenly over hot topping. Gently press chips into topping with spatula. Loosen caramel from edges of pan with a thin spatula or knife. Cool completely on wire rack. Cut into 3×1½-inch bars.   *Makes about 40 bars*

Triple Layer Chocolate Bars

1½ cups graham cracker crumbs
½ cup HERSHEY'S Cocoa
¼ cup sugar
⅓ cup margarine or butter, melted
1 (14-ounce) can EAGLE® Brand Sweetened
    Condensed Milk (NOT evaporated milk)
¼ cup flour
1 egg
1 teaspoon vanilla extract
½ teaspoon baking powder
¾ cup chopped nuts
1 (12-ounce) package HERSHEY'S Semi-Sweet
    Chocolate Chips

Preheat oven to 350°F. Combine crumbs, ¼ *cup* cocoa, sugar and margarine; press firmly on bottom of 13×9-inch baking pan.

In large bowl, beat sweetened condensed milk, flour, remaining ¼ *cup* cocoa, egg, vanilla and baking powder. Stir in nuts. Spread evenly over prepared crust. Top with chips. Bake 20 to 25 minutes or until set. Cool. Cut into bars. Store tightly covered at room temperature.   *Makes 24 to 36 bars*

Chocolate Caramel-Pecan Bars

Double Peanut-Choco Bars

1 (18¼- or 18½-ounce) package white cake
   mix
½ cup plus ⅓ cup peanut butter
1 egg
1 (14-ounce) can EAGLE® Brand Sweetened
   Condensed Milk (NOT evaporated milk)
1 (6-ounce) package semisweet chocolate chips
   (1 cup)
¾ cup Spanish peanuts

Preheat oven to 350°F (325°F for glass dish). In large mixer
bowl, combine cake mix, ½ *cup* peanut butter and egg; beat
on low speed until crumbly. Press firmly on bottom of greased
13×9-inch baking pan. In medium bowl, combine sweetened
condensed milk and remaining ⅓ *cup* peanut butter; mix well.
Spread evenly over prepared crust. Top with chips and peanuts.

Bake 30 to 35 minutes or until lightly browned. Cool. Cut into
bars. Store loosely covered at room temperature.

Makes 24 to 36 bars

Four-Layer Oatmeal Bars

OAT LAYER
½ BUTTER FLAVOR* CRISCO® Stick or ½ cup
   BUTTER FLAVOR* CRISCO® all-vegetable
   shortening
1 egg
1½ cups quick oats, uncooked
1 cup firmly packed brown sugar
¾ cup plus 2 tablespoons all-purpose flour
1 teaspoon cinnamon
¾ teaspoon baking soda
¼ teaspoon salt

FRUIT LAYER
1½ cups sliced, peeled fresh peaches**
   (cut slices in half crosswise)
¾ cup crushed pineapple, undrained
¾ cup sliced, peeled Granny Smith apple
   (cut slices in half crosswise)
½ cup chopped walnuts or pecans
¼ cup granulated sugar
2 tablespoons cornstarch
½ teaspoon nutmeg

CREAM CHEESE LAYER
1 (8-ounce) package cream cheese, softened
1 egg
¼ cup granulated sugar
½ teaspoon fresh lemon juice
½ teaspoon vanilla

*Butter Flavor Crisco is artificially flavored.

**Diced canned peaches, well drained, can be used in place of
fresh peaches.

1. Heat oven to 350°F. **Grease** 11×7-inch glass baking dish with shortening. **Place** cooling rack on countertop.

2. For oat layer, **combine** shortening and egg in large bowl. **Stir** with fork until blended. **Add** oats, brown sugar, flour, cinnamon, baking soda and salt. **Stir** until well blended and crumbs form. **Press** 1¾ cups crumbs lightly into bottom of prepared dish. **Reserve** remaining crumbs.

3. Bake at 350°F for 10 minutes. *Do not overbake.* **Cool** completely on cooling rack.

4. For fruit layer, **combine** peaches, pineapple, apple, nuts, granulated sugar, cornstarch and nutmeg in medium saucepan. **Cook** and stir over medium heat until mixture comes to a boil and thickens. **Cool** completely.

5. *Increase oven temperature to 375°F.*

6. For cream cheese layer, **combine** cream cheese, egg, granulated sugar, lemon juice and vanilla in medium bowl. **Beat** at medium speed of electric mixer until well blended. **Spread** over cooled oat layer. **Spoon** cooled fruit mixture over cheese layer. **Spread** gently to cover cream cheese. **Sprinkle** reserved crumbs over fruit.

7. Bake at 375°F for 30 minutes. *Do not overbake.* **Cool** to completely on cooling rack. **Refrigerate. Cut** into bars about 2×1¾ inches. *Makes about 20 bars*

Four-Layer Oatmeal Bars

Norwegian Almond Squares

1¾ cups all-purpose flour
1 cup sugar
¼ cup ground almonds
1 cup butter or margarine, softened
1 egg
1 teaspoon ground cinnamon
½ teaspoon salt
1 egg white
¾ cup sliced almonds

Preheat oven to 350°F. Combine flour, sugar, ground almonds, butter, egg, cinnamon and salt in large bowl. Beat at low speed of electric mixer, scraping bowl often, until well mixed, 2 to 3 minutes. Press dough onto ungreased cookie sheet to ¹⁄₁₆-inch thickness.

Beat egg white with fork in small bowl until foamy. Brush over dough; sprinkle with almonds. Bake 12 to 15 minutes or until very lightly browned. Immediately cut into 2-inch squares and remove from pan. Cool; store in tightly covered container.

Makes 36 to 48 squares

Almond Toffee Triangles

Bar Cookie Crust (page 67)
⅓ cup packed brown sugar
⅓ cup KARO® Light or Dark Corn Syrup
¼ cup MAZOLA® margarine
¼ cup heavy cream
1½ cups sliced almonds
1 teaspoon vanilla

Preheat oven to 350°F. Prepare Bar Cookie Crust according to recipe directions. In medium saucepan, combine brown sugar, corn syrup, margarine and cream. Bring to a boil over medium heat; remove from heat. Stir in almonds and vanilla. Pour over hot crust; spread evenly. Bake 15 to 20 minutes or until set and golden. Cool completely on wire rack. Cut into 2½-inch squares; cut each square in half diagonally to create triangles.

Makes about 48 triangles

Prep Time: 30 minutes
Bake Time: 20 minutes, *plus* cooling

Chewy Bar Cookies

½ cup margarine, softened
1 cup firmly packed light brown sugar
2 eggs
3 (1¼-ounce) packages Mix 'n Eat CREAM OF WHEAT® Cereal Apple 'n Cinnamon Flavor
⅔ cup all-purpose flour
2 teaspoons baking powder
1 cup PLANTERS® Walnuts, finely chopped

Preheat oven to 350°F. In large bowl, with electric mixer at medium speed, beat margarine and brown sugar until creamy. Beat in eggs until light and fluffy. Stir in cereal, flour and baking powder. Mix in walnuts. Spread batter in greased 15½×10½×1-inch baking pan.

Bake 20 to 25 minutes or until golden brown. Cool completely in pan on wire rack. Cut into bars.   *Makes about 48 bars*

Oatmeal Carmelita Bars

¾ BUTTER FLAVOR* CRISCO® Stick or ¾ cup
    BUTTER FLAVOR* CRISCO® all-vegetable
    shortening, melted
1½ cups quick oats (not instant or old
    fashioned), uncooked
¾ cup firmly packed brown sugar
½ cup plus 3 tablespoons all-purpose flour,
    divided
½ cup whole wheat flour
½ teaspoon baking soda
¼ teaspoon cinnamon
1⅓ cups milk chocolate chips
½ cup chopped walnuts
1 jar (12.5 ounces) or ¾ cup caramel ice cream
    topping

*Butter Flavor Crisco is artificially flavored.

1. Heat oven to 350°F. **Grease** bottom and sides of 9×9×2-inch baking pan with shortening. **Place** cooling rack on countertop.

2. Combine shortening, oats, sugar, ½ cup all-purpose flour, whole wheat flour, baking soda and cinnamon in large bowl. **Mix** at low speed of electric mixer until crumbs form. **Reserve** ½ cup for topping. **Press** remaining crumbs into prepared pan.

3. Bake at 350°F for 10 minutes. *Do not overbake.* **Sprinkle** chocolate chips and nuts over crust.

4. Combine caramel topping and remaining 3 tablespoons all-purpose flour. **Stir** until well blended. **Drizzle** over chocolate chips and nuts. **Sprinkle** reserved ½ cup crumbs over caramel topping.

5. Return to oven. **Bake** at 350°F for 20 to 25 minutes or until golden brown. *Do not overbake.* **Run** spatula around edge of pan before cooling. **Cool** completely in pan on cooling rack. **Cut** into 1½×1½-inch squares.

Makes 3 dozen squares

Chippy Cheeseys

BASE
1¼ cups firmly packed brown sugar
¾ BUTTER FLAVOR* CRISCO® Stick or ¾ cup
    BUTTER FLAVOR* CRISCO® all-vegetable
    shortening
2 tablespoons milk
1 tablespoon vanilla
1 egg
1¾ cups all-purpose flour
1 teaspoon salt
¾ teaspoon baking soda
1 cup semisweet mini chocolate chips
1 cup coarsely chopped walnuts
FILLING
2 (8-ounce) packages cream cheese, softened
2 eggs
¾ cup granulated sugar
1 teaspoon vanilla

*Butter Flavor Crisco is artificially flavored.

1. Heat oven to 375°F. **Grease** 13×9-inch pan with shortening. **Place** cooling rack on countertop for cooling cookies.

2. *For base,* **combine** brown sugar, shortening, milk and vanilla in large bowl. **Beat** at medium speed of electric mixer until well blended. **Beat** egg into shortening mixture.

3. Combine flour, salt and baking soda. **Mix** into shortening mixture just until blended. **Stir** in chocolate chips and walnuts. **Spread** half of dough in prepared pan.

4. Bake at 375°F for 8 minutes. *Do not overbake.*

5. *For filling,* **combine** cream cheese, eggs, granulated sugar and vanilla in medium bowl. **Beat** at medium speed of electric mixer until smooth. **Pour** over hot base.

6. Roll remaining half of dough into 13×9-inch rectangle between sheets of waxed paper. **Remove** top sheet. **Flip** dough over onto filling. **Remove** waxed paper.

7. Bake at 375°F for 40 minutes or until top is set and light golden brown. *Do not overbake.* **Cool** on cooling rack. **Cut** into 2×1¾-inch bars. **Refrigerate.**   *Makes about 30 bars*

Chippy Cheeseys

Chewy Oatmeal-Apricot-Date Bars

COOKIES

1¼ cups firmly packed brown sugar

¾ plus 4 teaspoons BUTTER FLAVOR* CRISCO®
    Stick or ¾ cup plus 4 teaspoons BUTTER
    FLAVOR* CRISCO® all-vegetable
    shortening

3 eggs

2 teaspoons vanilla

2 cups quick oats, uncooked, divided

½ cup all-purpose flour

2 teaspoons baking powder

1 teaspoon cinnamon

¼ teaspoon nutmeg

¼ teaspoon salt

1 cup finely grated carrots

1 cup finely minced dried apricots

1 cup minced dates

1 cup finely chopped walnuts

⅔ cup vanilla chips

FROSTING

1 (3-ounce) package cream cheese, softened

¼ BUTTER FLAVOR* CRISCO® Stick or ¼ cup
    BUTTER FLAVOR* CRISCO® all-vegetable
    shortening

2½ cups confectioners' sugar

1 to 2 teaspoons milk

¾ teaspoon lemon extract

½ teaspoon vanilla

½ teaspoon finely grated lemon peel

⅓ cup finely chopped walnuts

*Butter Flavor Crisco is artificially flavored.

1. Heat oven to 350°F. Grease 13×9-inch baking pan with shortening. **Flour** lightly. **Place** cooling rack on countertop.

2. For cookies, **combine** brown sugar and shortening in large bowl. **Beat** at medium speed of electric mixer until fluffy. **Add** eggs, 1 at a time, and 2 teaspoons vanilla. **Beat** until well blended and fluffy.

3. Process ½ cup oats in food processor or blender until finely ground. **Combine** ground oats with flour, baking powder, cinnamon, nutmeg and salt in medium bowl. **Add** oat mixture gradually to shortening mixture at low speed. **Add** remaining 1½ cups oats, carrots, apricots, dates, 1 cup nuts and vanilla chips. **Mix** until partially blended. **Finish** mixing with spoon. **Spread** in prepared pan.

4. Bake at 350°F for 35 to 45 minutes or until center is set and cookie starts to pull away from sides of pan. Toothpick inserted in center should come out clean. *Do not overbake.* **Cool** completely on cooling rack.

5. For frosting, **combine** cream cheese, ¼ cup shortening, confectioners' sugar, milk, lemon extract, ½ teaspoon vanilla and lemon peel in medium bowl. **Beat** at low speed until blended. **Increase** speed to medium-high. **Beat** until fluffy. **Stir** in ⅓ cup nuts. **Spread** on baked surface. **Cut** into bars about 2¼×2 inches. **Refrigerate.**

Makes about 24 bars

Breakfast Bars to Go

Breakfast Bars to Go

1 cup NABISCO® 100% Bran
⅔ cup applesauce
¾ cup chunky peanut butter
½ cup margarine
½ cup sugar
1 teaspoon vanilla extract
2 eggs
1 cup all-purpose flour
½ teaspoon baking soda
24 apple slices

Preheat oven to 350°F. In small bowl, combine bran and applesauce; let mixture stand 5 minutes.

In large bowl, with electric mixer at medium speed, blend peanut butter and margarine. Beat in sugar and vanilla. Add eggs, one at a time, beating 1 minute after each addition. Stir in bran mixture, flour and baking soda until well blended. Spread in greased and floured 13×9×2-inch baking pan. Arrange apple slices in 4 rows on top of batter.

Bake 25 to 30 minutes or until knife inserted in center comes out clean. Cool completely in pan on wire rack. Cut into bars. Store in airtight container. *Makes 24 bars*

Peanut Butter Bars

BASE
1¼ cups firmly packed light brown sugar
¾ cup creamy peanut butter
½ CRISCO® Stick or ½ cup CRISCO® all-vegetable shortening
3 tablespoons milk
1 tablespoon vanilla
2 eggs
1¾ cups all-purpose flour
1 cup quick oats, uncooked
¾ teaspoon salt
¾ teaspoon baking soda

PEANUT BUTTER LAYER
1½ cups confectioners' sugar
3 tablespoons milk
2 tablespoons creamy peanut butter
1 tablespoon BUTTER FLAVOR* CRISCO® Stick or 1 tablespoon BUTTER FLAVOR* CRISCO® all-vegetable shortening

CHOCOLATE GLAZE
2 squares (1 ounce each) unsweetened baking chocolate
2 tablespoons BUTTER FLAVOR* CRISCO® Stick or 2 tablespoons BUTTER FLAVOR* CRISCO® all-vegetable shortening

*Butter Flavor Crisco is artificially flavored.

1. Heat oven to 350°F. **Grease** 13×9-inch baking pan with shortening. **Place** cooling rack on countertop for cooling bars.

2. *For base,* **combine** brown sugar, peanut butter, shortening, milk and vanilla in large bowl. **Beat** at medium speed of electric mixer until blended. **Add** eggs. **Beat** just until blended.

3. Combine flour, oats, salt and baking soda. **Add** to shortening mixture at low speed. **Mix** just until blended. **Press** into prepared pan.

4. Bake at 350°F for 20 minutes or until golden brown. *Do not overbake.* **Cool** completely on cooling rack.

5. *For peanut butter layer,* **combine** confectioners sugar, milk, peanut butter and shortening. **Mix** with spoon until smooth. **Spread** on cooled base. **Refrigerate** 30 minutes.

6. *For chocolate glaze,* **combine** chocolate and shortening in microwave-safe bowl. **Microwave** at 50% (MEDIUM). **Stir** after 1 minute. **Repeat** until smooth or melt on rangetop in small saucepan on very low heat. **Cool** slightly. **Spread** over peanut butter layer. **Cut** into bars about 3×1½ inches. **Refrigerate** about 1 hour or until set. **Let** stand 15 to 20 minutes at room temperature before serving.

Makes about 3 dozen cookies

After School Treats

Chocolate Peanut Butter Cookies

1 package **DUNCAN HINES**® Moist Deluxe Devil's Food Cake Mix

¾ cup **JIF**® Extra Crunchy Peanut Butter

2 eggs

2 tablespoons milk

1 cup candy-coated peanut butter pieces

1. Preheat oven to 350°F. Grease cookie sheets.

2. Combine cake mix, peanut butter, eggs and milk in large bowl. Mix at low speed with electric mixer until blended. Stir in peanut butter pieces.

3. Drop dough by slightly rounded tablespoonfuls onto prepared cookie sheets. Bake 7 to 9 minutes or until lightly browned. Cool 2 minutes on cookie sheets. Remove to cooling racks.

Makes about 3½ dozen cookies

Tip: You can use 1 cup peanut butter chips in place of peanut butter pieces.

Peanut Butter and Chocolate Cookie Sandwich Cookies

  ½ cup REESE'S® Peanut Butter Chips
  3 tablespoons plus ½ cup butter or margarine,
    softened and divided
1¼ cups sugar, divided
  ¼ cup light corn syrup
  1 egg
  1 teaspoon vanilla extract
  2 cups plus 2 tablespoons all-purpose flour,
    divided
  2 teaspoons baking soda
  ¼ teaspoon salt
  ½ cup HERSHEY'S Cocoa
  5 tablespoons butter or margarine, melted
    Additional sugar for rolling
    About 2 dozen large marshmallows

Heat oven to 350°F. In small saucepan over very low heat, melt peanut butter chips and 3 tablespoons softened butter. Remove from heat; cool slightly.

In large bowl, beat remaining ½ cup softened butter and 1 cup sugar until light and fluffy. Add corn syrup, egg and vanilla; blend thoroughly. Stir together 2 cups flour, baking soda and salt; add to butter mixture, blending well. Remove 1¼ cups batter and place in small bowl. With wooden spoon, stir in the remaining 2 tablespoons flour and peanut butter chip mixture.

Blend cocoa, remaining ¼ cup sugar and 5 tablespoons melted butter into remaining batter. Refrigerate both batters 5 to 10 minutes or until firm enough to handle. Roll each dough into 1-inch balls; roll in sugar. Place on ungreased cookie sheets.

Bake 10 to 11 minutes or until set. Cool slightly; remove from cookie sheets to wire racks. Cool completely. Place 1 marshmallow on flat side of 1 chocolate cookie. Microwave at MEDIUM (50%) 10 seconds or until marshmallow is softened. Place a peanut butter cookie over marshmallow, pressing down slightly. Repeat with remaining cookies. Serve immediately.

Makes about 2 dozen cookie sandwiches

Peanut Butter Chip Brownies

  ½ cup butter or margarine
  4 squares (1 ounce each) semisweet chocolate
  ½ cup sugar
  2 eggs
  1 teaspoon vanilla
  ½ cup all-purpose flour
  1 package (12 ounces) peanut butter chips
  1 cup (6 ounces) milk chocolate chips

Preheat oven to 350°F. Grease 8-inch square baking pan. Melt butter and semisweet chocolate in small, heavy saucepan over low heat, stirring just until chocolate melts. Remove from heat; cool. Beat sugar and eggs in large bowl until light and fluffy. Blend in vanilla and chocolate mixture. Stir in flour until blended; fold in peanut butter chips. Spread batter evenly in prepared pan.

Bake 25 to 30 minutes or just until firm and dry in center. Remove from oven; sprinkle milk chocolate chips over top. Place pan on wire rack. When chocolate chips have melted, spread over brownies. Refrigerate until chocolate topping is set. Cut into 2-inch squares. *Makes 16 brownies*

Cheery Chocolate Teddy Bear Cookies

1 (10-ounce) package REESE'S® Peanut Butter Chips

1 cup (6 ounces) HERSHEY'S Semi-Sweet Chocolate Chips

2 tablespoons shortening (do not use butter, margarine or oil)

1 (20-ounce) package chocolate sandwich cookies

1 (10-ounce) package teddy bear shaped graham snack crackers

Line trays or cookie sheets with waxed paper. In 2-quart glass measuring cup with handle, combine chips and shortening. Microwave on HIGH (100% power) 1½ to 2 minutes or until chips are melted and mixture is smooth when stirred. With fork, dip each cookie into melted chip mixture; gently tap fork on side of cup to remove excess chocolate. Place chocolate-coated cookies on prepared trays; top each cookie with a graham snack cracker. Chill until chocolate is set, about 30 minutes. Store in airtight container in a cool, dry place.

Makes about 4 dozen cookies

Chocolatey Peanut Butter Goodies

COOKIES

1 BUTTER FLAVOR* CRISCO® Stick or 1 cup BUTTER FLAVOR* CRISCO® all-vegetable shortening

4 cups powdered sugar

1½ cups extra crunchy peanut butter

1½ cups graham cracker crumbs

FROSTING

1 tablespoon BUTTER FLAVOR* CRISCO® Stick or 1 tablespoon BUTTER FLAVOR* CRISCO® all-vegetable shortening

1⅓ cups semisweet chocolate chips

*Butter Flavor Crisco is artificially flavored.

1. For cookies, **combine** shortening, powdered sugar, peanut butter and crumbs in large bowl with spoon. **Spread** evenly on bottom of 13×9-inch baking pan.

2. For frosting, **combine** shortening and chocolate chips in small microwave-safe bowl. **Microwave** at MEDIUM (50%). Stir after 1 minute. **Repeat** until smooth (or melt on rangetop in small saucepan on very low heat). **Spread** over top of cookie mixture. **Cool** at least 1 hour or until chocolate hardens. **Cut** into 2×1½-inch bars.

Makes about 3 dozen bars

"Radical" Peanut Butter Pizza Cookies

COOKIES
- 1 BUTTER FLAVOR* CRISCO® Stick or 1 cup BUTTER FLAVOR* CRISCO® all-vegetable shortening
- 1¼ cups granulated sugar, divided
- 1 cup packed dark brown sugar
- 1 cup creamy peanut butter
- 2 eggs
- 1 teaspoon baking soda
- 1 teaspoon vanilla
- ½ teaspoon salt
- 2 cups all-purpose flour
- 2 cups quick oats, uncooked

PIZZA SAUCE
- 2 cups milk chocolate chips
- ¼ BUTTER FLAVOR* CRISCO® Stick or ¼ cup BUTTER FLAVOR* CRISCO® all-vegetable shortening

PIZZA TOPPING (any of the following)
- Mmmmm—candy coated chocolate pieces
- Beary good—gummy bears
- Jumbo jewels—small pieces of gumdrops
- Harvest mix—candy corn and chopped peanuts
- Ants and logs—cashews and raisins

DRIZZLE
- 1 cup chopped white confectionery coating

*Butter Flavor Crisco is artificially flavored.

"Radical" Peanut Butter Pizza Cookies

1. Heat oven to 350°F. **Place** sheets of foil on countertop for cooling cookies.

2. For cookies, **combine** shortening, 1 cup granulated sugar and brown sugar in large bowl. **Beat** at low speed of electric mixer until well blended. **Add** peanut butter, eggs, baking soda, vanilla and salt. **Mix** about 2 minutes or until well blended. **Stir** in flour and oats.

3. Place remaining ¼ cup granulated sugar in small bowl.

4. Measure ¼ cup dough. **Shape** into ball. **Repeat** with remaining dough. **Roll** each ball in sugar. **Place** 5 inches apart on ungreased baking sheets. **Flatten** into 4-inch circles.

5. Bake one baking sheet at a time at 350°F for 8 to 10 minutes. *Do not overbake.* **Use** back of spoon to flatten center and up to edge of each hot cookie to resemble pizza crust. **Cool** 5 to 8 minutes on baking sheets. **Remove** cookies to foil to cool completely.

6. For pizza sauce, **combine** chocolate chips and shortening in large microwave-safe measuring cup or bowl. **Microwave** at MEDIUM (50%) for 2 to 3 minutes or until chips are shiny and soft (or melt on rangetop in small saucepan on very low heat). **Stir** until smooth. **Spoon** 2 teaspoons melted chocolate into center of each cookie. **Spread** to inside edge. **Sprinkle** desired toppings over chocolate.

7. For drizzle, **place** chopped confectionery coating in heavy resealable plastic food storage bag. **Seal. Microwave** at MEDIUM (50%). **Knead** bag after 1 minute. **Repeat** until smooth (or melt by placing in bowl of hot water). **Cut** pinpoint hole in corner of bag. **Squeeze** out and drizzle over cookies.

Makes about 2 dozen cookies

Peanut Butter Chips and Jelly Bars

 1½ cups all-purpose flour
 ½ cup sugar
 ¾ teaspoon baking powder
 ½ cup cold butter or margarine
 1 egg, beaten
 ¾ cup grape jelly
 1 cup REESE'S® Peanut Butter Chips, divided

Preheat oven to 375°F. Grease 9-inch square baking pan. In medium bowl, combine flour, sugar and baking powder; cut in butter with pastry blender or 2 knives to form coarse crumbs. Add egg; blend well. Reserve half of crumb mixture; press remaining half of mixture onto bottom of prepared pan. Spread jelly evenly over crust. Sprinkle ½ cup peanut butter chips over jelly. Combine remaining ½ of crumb mixture with remaining ½ cup chips; sprinkle over top. Bake 25 to 30 minutes or until lightly browned. Cool completely. Cut into bars.

Makes about 18 bars

Peanut Butter Bears

1 cup SKIPPY® Creamy Peanut Butter
1 cup MAZOLA® Margarine, softened
1 cup packed brown sugar
⅔ cup KARO® Light or Dark Corn Syrup
2 eggs
4 cups all-purpose flour, divided
1 tablespoon baking powder
1 teaspoon cinnamon (optional)
¼ teaspoon salt

In large bowl, with mixer at medium speed, beat peanut butter, margarine, brown sugar, corn syrup and eggs until smooth. Reduce speed to low; beat in 2 cups flour, baking powder, cinnamon and salt. With spoon, stir in remaining 2 cups flour. Wrap dough in plastic wrap; refrigerate 2 hours.

Preheat oven to 325°F. Divide dough in half; set aside one half. On floured surface roll out half the dough to ⅛-inch thickness. Cut with floured bear cookie cutter. Repeat with remaining dough. Bake on ungreased cookie sheets 10 minutes or until lightly browned. Remove from cookie sheets; cool completely on wire racks. Decorate as desired.

Makes about 3 dozen bears

Prep Time: 35 minutes, plus chilling
Bake Time: 10 minutes, plus cooling

Note: *Use scraps of dough to make bear faces. Make one small ball of dough for muzzle. Form 3 smaller balls of dough and press gently to create eyes and nose; bake as directed. If desired, use frosting to create paws, ears and bow ties.*

Peanut Butter Cremes

¾ BUTTER FLAVOR* CRISCO® Stick or ¾ cup
     BUTTER FLAVOR* CRISCO® all-vegetable
     shortening
1 cup creamy peanut butter
1 cup packed dark brown sugar
1 cup marshmallow creme
1 egg
2 teaspoons vanilla
1¾ cups all-purpose flour
1 teaspoon baking powder
1 teaspoon salt

*Butter Flavor Crisco is artificially flavored.

1. Heat oven to 350°F. **Place** sheets of foil on countertop for cooling cookies.

2. Combine shortening, peanut butter, brown sugar and marshmallow creme in large bowl. **Beat** at medium speed of electric mixer until well blended. **Beat** in egg and vanilla.

3. Combine flour, baking powder and salt. **Mix** into shortening mixture at low speed until just blended.

4. Drop by rounded tablespoonfuls 2 inches apart onto ungreased baking sheets.

5. Bake one baking sheet at a time at 350°F for 11 minutes or until lightly browned. *Do not overbake.* **Cool** 2 minutes on baking sheets. **Remove** cookies to foil to cool completely.

Makes about 4 dozen cookies

Peanut Butter Bears

Chewy Choco-Peanut Pudgies

COOKIES

1¼ cups firmly packed light brown sugar
¾ cup creamy peanut butter
½ CRISCO® Stick or ½ cup CRISCO®
    all-vegetable shortening
3 tablespoons milk
1 tablespoon vanilla
1 egg
1¾ cups all-purpose flour
¾ teaspoon salt
¾ teaspoon baking soda
1½ cups coarsely chopped unsalted peanuts
    (raw or dry roasted)
½ cup granulated sugar

FROSTING

½ cup semisweet chocolate chips
½ teaspoon BUTTER FLAVOR* CRISCO® Stick
    or ½ teaspoon BUTTER FLAVOR* CRISCO®
    all-vegetable shortening
½ teaspoon granulated sugar

* Butter Flavor Crisco is artificially flavored.

1. Heat oven to 375°F. **Place** sheets of foil on countertop for cooling cookies.

2. *For cookies,* **combine** brown sugar, peanut butter, shortening, milk and vanilla in large bowl. **Beat** at medium speed of electric mixer until well blended. **Add** egg. **Beat** just until blended.

3. Combine flour, salt and baking soda. **Add** to shortening mixture at low speed. **Mix** just until blended. **Stir** in nuts.

4. Form dough into 1¼-inch balls. **Roll** in granulated sugar. **Place** 2 inches apart onto ungreased baking sheets.

5. Bake one baking sheet at a time at 375°F for 7 to 8 minutes or until set and just beginning to brown. *Do not overbake.* **Cool** 2 minutes on baking sheets. **Remove** cookies to foil to cool completely.

6. *For frosting,* **combine** chocolate chips, shortening and granulated sugar in microwave-safe measuring cup. Microwave at 50% (MEDIUM). **Stir** after 1 minute. **Repeat** until smooth (or melt on rangetop in small saucepan on very low heat). **Drizzle** generously over cooled cookies.

Makes about 3 dozen cookies

Peanut Butter Stars

Peanut Butter Stars

1 package DUNCAN HINES® Peanut Butter
    Cookie Mix
1 egg
¼ cup CRISCO® Oil or CRISCO® PURITAN®
    Canola Oil
1 package (3½ ounces) chocolate sprinkles
1 package (7 ounces) milk chocolate candy
    stars

1. Preheat oven to 375°F.

2. Combine cookie mix, contents of peanut butter packet from Mix, egg and oil in large bowl. Stir until thoroughly blended. Shape dough into 1-inch balls. Roll in chocolate sprinkles. Place 2 inches apart onto ungreased baking sheets. Bake at 375°F for 8 to 10 minutes or until set. Immediately place milk chocolate candy stars on top of hot cookies. Cool 1 minute on baking sheets. Remove to cooling racks. Cool completely. Store in airtight containers.   *Makes 4½ to 5 dozen cookies*

Tip: *For evenly baked cookies, place baking sheet in center of oven, not touching the sides.*

Oatmeal-Chocolate Raisin Cookies

¾ **BUTTER FLAVOR* CRISCO®** Stick or ¾ cup
    BUTTER FLAVOR* CRISCO® all-vegetable
    shortening
1¼ cups firmly packed light brown sugar
  1 egg
  ⅓ cup milk
1½ teaspoons vanilla
  3 cups quick oats, uncooked
  1 cup all-purpose flour
  ½ teaspoon baking soda
  ½ teaspoon salt
  ¼ teaspoon cinnamon
  2 cups chocolate-covered raisins
  1 cup coarsely chopped pecans

*Butter Flavor Crisco is artificially flavored.

1. Heat oven to 375°F. **Grease** baking sheets with shortening. **Place** sheets of foil on countertop for cooling cookies.

2. Combine shortening, brown sugar, egg, milk and vanilla in large bowl. **Beat** at medium speed of electric mixer until well blended.

3. Combine oats, flour, baking soda, salt and cinnamon. **Mix** into shortening mixture at low speed until just blended. **Stir** in raisins and nuts.

4. Drop by rounded measuring tablespoonfuls 2 inches apart onto prepared baking sheets.

5. Bake one baking sheet at a time at 375°F for 10 to 12 minutes or until lightly browned. *Do not overbake.* **Cool** 2 minutes on baking sheets. **Remove** cookies to foil to cool completely.   *Makes about 2½ dozen cookies*

Whole-Wheat Oatmeal Cookies

  1 cup whole-wheat flour
  1 teaspoon ground cinnamon
  1 teaspoon baking powder
  ½ teaspoon baking soda
  ½ teaspoon salt
  1 cup packed light brown sugar
  ¼ cup unsweetened applesauce
  2 egg whites
  2 tablespoons margarine
1½ teaspoons vanilla
1⅓ cups rolled oats, uncooked
  ½ cup raisins

Preheat oven to 375°F. Lightly spray cookie sheets with nonstick cooking spray. Set aside.

Combine flour, cinnamon, baking powder, baking soda and salt in medium bowl; mix well. Combine brown sugar, applesauce, egg whites, margarine and vanilla in large bowl. Mix until small crumbs form. Add flour mixture; blend well. Blend in oats and raisins.

Drop by rounded teaspoonfuls onto prepared cookie sheets, 2 inches apart. Bake 10 to 12 minutes or until golden brown. Cool on wire racks.   *Makes 3½ dozen cookies*

Oatmeal Shaggies Cookies

COOKIES

2 cups quick oats, uncooked
1 cup finely shredded carrots
1 cup firmly packed brown sugar
1 cup raisins
1 cup all-purpose flour
1 teaspoon baking powder
1 teaspoon baking soda
1 teaspoon salt
½ teaspoon ground cinnamon
½ teaspoon crushed cloves
2 eggs, beaten
½ **BUTTER FLAVOR* CRISCO® Stick** or ½ cup
    BUTTER FLAVOR* CRISCO® all-vegetable
    shortening, melted and cooled
⅓ cup milk
1 cup shredded coconut
½ cup finely chopped walnuts

FROSTING

1 cup confectioners' sugar
2 tablespoons butter or margarine, softened
2 teaspoons grated orange peel
1 tablespoon plus 1 teaspoon orange juice

*Butter Flavor Crisco is artificially flavored.

Oatmeal Shaggies Cookies

1. Heat oven to 350°F. Grease baking sheets with shortening. **Place** sheets of foil on countertop for cooling cookies.

2. For cookies, **combine** oats, carrots, brown sugar and raisins in large bowl.

3. Combine flour, baking powder, baking soda, salt, cinnamon and cloves. **Stir** into oat mixture with spoon.

4. Combine eggs, shortening and milk. **Stir** into oat mixture. **Stir** in coconut and nuts. **Drop** by rounded tablespoonfuls 2½ inches apart onto greased baking sheets.

5. Bake one baking sheet at a time at 350°F for 10 to 12 minutes or until lightly browned. *Do not overbake.* **Cool** on baking sheets 2 minutes. **Remove** cookies to foil to cool completely.

6. For frosting, **combine** confectioners' sugar, butter, orange peel and orange juice in small bowl. **Stir** until smooth and of desired spreading consistency. **Frost** cookies.

Makes 2½ to 3 dozen cookies

Cocoa Kiss Cookies

 1 cup butter or margarine, softened
 ⅔ cup sugar
 1 teaspoon vanilla
 1⅔ cups unsifted all-purpose flour
 ¼ cup HERSHEY₀S Cocoa
 1 cup finely chopped pecans
 1 (9-ounce package) HERSHEY₀S KISSES® Milk
   Chocolates (about 54)
 Confectioners' sugar

Preheat oven to 350°F. Beat butter, sugar and vanilla in large bowl until light and fluffy. Combine flour and cocoa; blend into butter mixture. Add pecans; beat on low speed until well blended. Chill dough 1 hour or until firm enough to handle. Remove and discard wrappers from chocolate pieces.

Shape scant tablespoon of dough around each chocolate piece, covering completely; shape into balls. Place on ungreased cookie sheets. Bake 10 to 12 minutes or until almost set. Cool slightly. Remove from cookie sheets; cool completely on wire racks. Roll in confectioners' sugar.

Makes about 4½ dozen cookies

Chocolate Candy Cookies

 ⅔ cup MIRACLE WHIP® Salad Dressing
 1 two-layer devil's food cake mix
 2 eggs
 1 (8-ounce) package candy-coated chocolate
   candies

• Preheat oven to 375°F.

• Blend salad dressing, cake mix and eggs at low speed with electric mixer until moistened. Beat on medium speed 2 minutes. Stir in chocolate candies. (Dough will be stiff.)

• Drop by rounded teaspoonfuls, 2 inches apart, onto greased cookie sheets.

• Bake 9 to 11 minutes or until almost set. (Cookies will still appear soft.) Cool 1 minute; remove from cookie sheets.

Makes about 4½ dozen cookies

Candy Shop Pizza

1 package (18 ounces) NESTLÉ® Refrigerated
    Chocolate Chip Cookie Dough or Chocolate
    Chocolate Chip Cookie Dough or Sugar
    Cookie Dough with Butterfinger® Pieces
1 cup NESTLÉ® Toll House® Semi-Sweet
    Chocolate Morsels
½ cup peanut butter
1 cup coarsely chopped assorted NESTLÉ®
    candy such as Butterfinger® bars, Crunch®
    bars, Baby Ruth® bars, Goobers® or
    Raisinets®

Press cookie dough evenly into bottom of greased 12-inch pizza pan or 13×9-inch baking pan.

Bake in preheated 350°F oven for 14 to 18 minutes or until edge is set and center is still slightly soft. Immediately sprinkle morsels over hot crust; drop peanut butter by spoonfuls onto morsels. Let stand for 5 minutes or until morsels become shiny and soft. Gently spread chocolate and peanut butter evenly over cookie crust.

Sprinkle candy in single layer over pizza. Cut into wedges; serve warm or at room temperature.

Makes about 12 servings

MILKY WAY® Bar Cookies

3 MARS® MILKY WAY® Bars (2.15 ounces
    each), chopped, divided
2 tablespoons milk
½ cup butter or margarine, softened
⅓ cup packed light brown sugar
1 egg
½ teaspoon vanilla extract
1⅔ cups all-purpose flour
½ teaspoon baking soda
¼ teaspoon salt
½ cup chopped walnuts

Preheat oven to 350°F. Stir 1 MARS® MILKY WAY® Bar with milk in small saucepan over low heat until melted and smooth; cool. In large bowl, beat butter and brown sugar until creamy. Beat in egg, vanilla and melted MARS® MILKY WAY® Bar mixture. Combine flour, baking soda and salt in small bowl. Stir into chocolate mixture. Add remaining chopped MARS® MILKY WAY® Bars and nuts; stir gently. Drop dough by rounded teaspoonfuls onto ungreased cookie sheets.

Bake 12 to 15 minutes or until cookies are just firm to the touch. Cool on wire racks.   *Makes about 2 dozen cookies*

Prep time: 20 minutes
Bake time: 15 minutes

Chewy Fingers

¾ BUTTER FLAVOR* CRISCO® Stick or ¾ cup
    BUTTER FLAVOR* CRISCO® all-vegetable
    shortening
1¼ cups firmly packed light brown sugar
 1 egg
⅓ cup milk
1½ teaspoons vanilla
 3 cups quick oats, uncooked
 1 cup all-purpose flour
½ teaspoon baking soda
½ teaspoon salt
¾ cup semisweet chocolate chips
 2 BUTTERFINGER® candy bars (2.1 ounces
    each), cut into ¼-inch pieces

* Butter Flavor Crisco is artificially flavored.

1. Heat oven to 375°F. **Grease** baking sheets with shortening. **Place** sheets of foil on countertop for cooling cookies.

2. Combine shortening, brown sugar, egg, milk and vanilla in large bowl. **Beat** at medium speed of electric mixer until well blended.

3. Combine oats, flour, baking soda and salt. **Mix** into shortening mixture at low speed just until blended. **Stir** in chips and candy pieces.

4. Form dough into 1-inch balls. **Place** 2 inches apart onto prepared baking sheets.

5. Bake one baking sheet at a time at 375°F for 10 to 12 minutes or until lightly browned. *Do not overbake.* **Cool** 2 minutes on baking sheets. **Remove** cookies to foil to cool completely.　　　　*Makes about 2½ dozen cookies*

Brownie Candy Cups

1 package DUNCAN HINES® Chocolate Lovers'
    EXXTRA Double Fudge Brownie Mix
 2 eggs
⅓ cup water
¼ cup CRISCO® Oil or CRISCO® PURITAN®
    Canola Oil
30 miniature peanut butter cup candies,
    wrappers removed

1. Preheat oven to 350°F. Place 30 (2-inch) foil liners in muffin pans or on cookie sheets.

2. Combine brownie mix, fudge packet from Mix, eggs, water and oil in large bowl. Stir with spoon until well blended, about 50 strokes. Place 2 level measuring tablespoons batter in each foil liner. Bake at 350°F for 10 minutes. Remove from oven. Push 1 peanut butter cup candy in center of each cupcake until even with surface of brownie. Bake 5 to 7 minutes. Remove to cooling racks. Cool completely.　　　*Makes 30 brownie cups*

Orange Drop Cookies

COOKIES
- 1 package DUNCAN HINES® Golden Sugar Cookie Mix
- 2 eggs
- ⅓ cup CRISCO® Oil or CRISCO® PURITAN® Canola Oil
- 1 tablespoon orange juice
- ½ teaspoon grated orange peel
- ¾ cup flaked coconut
- ½ cup chopped pecans

GLAZE
- 1½ cups confectioners' sugar
- 1 tablespoon lemon juice
- 1 tablespoon orange juice
- 1½ teaspoons grated orange peel

1. Preheat oven to 375°F.

2. For cookies, combine cookie mix, eggs, 1 tablespoon orange juice and ½ teaspoon orange peel in large bowl. Stir with spoon until well blended. Stir in coconut and pecans. Drop by rounded teaspoonfuls 2 inches apart onto ungreased cookie sheets. Bake at 375°F for 7 to 8 minutes or until set. Cool 1 minute on cookie sheets. Remove to cooling racks. Cool completely.

3. For glaze, combine confectioners' sugar, lemon juice, 1 tablespoon orange juice and 1½ teaspoons orange peel in small bowl. Stir until blended. Drizzle over top of cooled cookies. Allow glaze to set before storing between layers of waxed paper in airtight container.

Makes about 4 dozen cookies

Raspberry Freckles

COOKIES
- 1 cup sugar
- ½ BUTTER FLAVOR* CRISCO® Stick or ½ cup BUTTER FLAVOR* CRISCO® all-vegetable shortening
- 1 egg
- 1 tablespoon raspberry-flavored liqueur
- 2⅔ cups all-purpose flour
- 1 teaspoon baking powder
- ½ teaspoon baking soda
- ½ teaspoon salt
- ½ cup sour cream
- 1 cup cubed (⅛- to ¼-inch) white confectionery coating
- ¾ cup mini semisweet chocolate chips
- ½ cup (2¼-ounce bag) crushed, sliced almonds

TOPPING
- ¼ cup seedless red raspberry jam
- 1 teaspoon raspberry-flavored liqueur
- ⅓ cup chopped white confectionery coating
- 2 teaspoons BUTTER FLAVOR* CRISCO® Stick or 2 teaspoons BUTTER FLAVOR* CRISCO® all-vegetable shortening

*Butter Flavor Crisco is artificially flavored.

1. Heat oven to 375°F. **Grease** baking sheets with shortening. **Place** sheets of foil on countertop for cooling cookies.

2. For cookies, **combine** sugar and shortening in large bowl. **Stir** with spoon until well blended. **Stir** in egg and 1 tablespoon liqueur.

3. Combine flour, baking powder, baking soda and salt. **Add** alternately with sour cream to shortening mixture. **Stir** in cubed confectionery coating, chocolate chips and almonds.

4. Roll dough to ¼-inch thickness on floured surface. **Cut** with 3-inch scalloped round cutter. **Place** 2 inches apart on prepared baking sheets.

5. Bake one baking sheet at a time at 375°F for 7 minutes or just until beginning to brown. *Do not overbake.* **Cool** 2 minutes on baking sheets. **Remove** cookies to foil to cool completely.

6. For topping, **combine** raspberry jam and 1 teaspoon liqueur in microwave-safe measuring cup or bowl. **Microwave** at MEDIUM (50%) until jam melts (or melt on rangetop in small saucepan on very low heat). **Drop** mixture in 10 to 12 dots to resemble freckles on top of each cookie.

7. Combine chopped confectionery coating and 2 teaspoons shortening in heavy resealable plastic food storage bag. **Seal. Microwave** at MEDIUM (50%). **Knead** bag after 1 minute. **Repeat** until smooth (or melt by placing in bowl of hot water). **Cut** pinpoint hole in corner of bag. **Squeeze** out and drizzle over cookies.   *Makes about 3 dozen cookies*

Raspberry Freckles

Cocoa Almond Cut-Out Cookies

¾ cup margarine or butter, softened
1 (14-ounce) can EAGLE® Brand Sweetened
   Condensed Milk (NOT evaporated milk)
2 eggs
1 teaspoon vanilla extract
½ teaspoon almond extract
2¾ cups unsifted flour
⅔ cup HERSHEY®'S Cocoa
2 teaspoons baking powder
½ teaspoon baking soda
½ cup finely chopped almonds
   Chocolate Glaze (recipe follows)

In large bowl, beat margarine, sweetened condensed milk, eggs and extracts until well blended. In another large bowl combine flour, cocoa, baking powder and baking soda; add to margarine mixture. Beat until well blended. Stir in almonds. Divide dough into 4 equal portions. Wrap each portion in plastic wrap; flatten. Chill until firm enough to roll, about 2 hours.

Preheat oven to 350°F. Working with 1 portion at a time (keep remaining dough in refrigerator), on floured surface, roll to about ⅛-inch thickness. Cut into desired shapes. Place on lightly greased cookie sheets. Bake 6 to 8 minutes or until set. Remove to wire racks; cool completely. Drizzle with Chocolate Glaze. Store tightly covered at room temperature.

Makes about 6 dozen 3-inch cookies

Chocolate Glaze: Melt 1 cup (6 ounces) HERSHEY®'S Semi-Sweet Chocolate Chips with 2 tablespoons shortening. Makes about ⅔ cup.

Cocoa Almond Cut-Out Cookies

Cowboy Macaroons

¾ BUTTER FLAVOR* CRISCO® Stick or ¾ cup
    BUTTER FLAVOR* CRISCO® all-vegetable
    shortening
1¼ cups firmly packed light brown sugar
  1 egg
 ⅓ cup milk
1½ teaspoons vanilla
1½ cups quick oats, uncooked
1½ cups corn flakes
  1 cup all-purpose flour
 ½ teaspoon baking soda
 ½ teaspoon salt
 ¼ teaspoon cinnamon
  1 cup coarsely chopped walnuts
 ¾ cup finely chopped pecans
 ¾ cup flake coconut
 ⅓ cup maraschino cherries, cut into quarters
    (optional)

* Butter Flavor Crisco is artificially flavored.

1. Heat oven to 375°F. **Grease** baking sheets with shortening. **Place** sheets of foil on countertop for cooling cookies.

2. Combine shortening, brown sugar, egg, milk and vanilla in large bowl. **Beat** at medium speed of electric mixer until well blended.

3. Combine oats, corn flakes, flour, baking soda, salt and cinnamon. **Mix** into shortening mixture at low speed just until blended. **Stir** in nuts, coconut and cherries.

4. Form dough into 1-inch balls. **Place** 2 inches apart onto prepared baking sheets.

5. Bake one baking sheet at a time at 375°F for 10 to 12 minutes or until lightly browned. *Do not overbake.* **Cool** 2 minutes on baking sheets. **Remove** cookies to foil to cool completely.   *Makes about 3 dozen cookies*

Giant Raisin-Chip Frisbees

  1 cup butter or margarine, softened
  1 cup packed brown sugar
 ½ cup granulated sugar
  2 eggs
  1 teaspoon vanilla
1½ cups all-purpose flour
 ¼ cup unsweetened cocoa powder
  1 teaspoon baking soda
  1 cup (6 ounces) semisweet chocolate chips
 ¾ cup raisins
 ¾ cup chopped walnuts

Preheat oven to 350°F. Line cookie sheets with parchment paper or lightly grease and dust with flour.

Beat butter and both sugars in large bowl. Add eggs and vanilla; beat until light. Combine flour, cocoa and baking soda in small bowl. Add to butter mixture with chocolate chips, raisins and walnuts; stir until well blended.

Scoop out about ½ cup of dough for each cookie. Place on prepared cookie sheets, spacing about 5 inches apart. Using knife dipped in water, smooth balls of dough out to about 3½ inches in diameter. Bake 10 to 12 minutes or until golden. Remove to wire racks to cool.   *Makes about 16 cookies*

Granola Bars

        3 cups quick-cooking oats, uncooked
        1 cup peanuts
        1 cup raisins
        1 cup sunflower seeds, shells removed
    1½ teaspoons ground cinnamon
        1 (14-ounce) can EAGLE® Brand Sweetened
            Condensed Milk (NOT evaporated milk)
        ½ cup margarine or butter, melted

Preheat oven to 325°F. Line 15×10-inch baking pan with foil; grease. In large bowl, combine oats, peanuts, raisins, sunflower seeds, cinnamon, sweetened condensed milk and margarine; mix well. Press evenly into prepared pan. Bake 25 to 30 minutes or until golden brown. Cool slightly; remove from pan and peel off foil. Cut into bars. Store loosely covered at room temperature.   *Makes 36 to 48 bars*

Granola Bars

Granola & Chocolate Chip Cookies

    1¼ cups firmly packed light brown sugar
        ¾ BUTTER FLAVOR* CRISCO® Stick or ¾ cup
            BUTTER FLAVOR* CRISCO® all-vegetable
            shortening
        2 tablespoons milk
        1 tablespoon vanilla
        1 egg
    1¼ cups all-purpose flour
        1 teaspoon salt
        ¾ teaspoon baking soda
        2 cups granola cereal
        1 cup semisweet chocolate chips

* Butter Flavor Crisco is artificially flavored.

1. Heat oven to 375°F. **Place** sheets of foil on countertop for cooling cookies.

2. Combine brown sugar, shortening, milk and vanilla in large bowl. **Beat** at medium speed of electric mixer until well blended. **Beat** egg into shortening mixture.

3. Combine flour, salt and baking soda. **Mix** into shortening mixture just until blended. **Stir** in granola and chocolate chips.

4. Drop by rounded measuring tablespoonfuls of dough 3 inches apart onto ungreased baking sheets.

5. Bake one baking sheet at a time at 375°F for 8 to 10 minutes for chewy cookies, or 11 to 13 minutes for crisp cookies. *Do not overbake.* **Cool** 2 minutes on baking sheets. **Remove** cookies to foil to cool completely.

Makes about 3½ dozen cookies

Corn Flake Macaroons

    4 egg whites
    ¼ teaspoon cream of tartar
    1 teaspoon vanilla
1⅓ cups sugar
    1 cup chopped pecans
    1 cup shredded coconut
    3 cups KELLOGG'S® CORN FLAKES® Cereal

1. Preheat oven to 325°F. In large bowl, beat egg whites until foamy. Stir in cream of tartar and vanilla. Gradually add sugar, beating until stiff and glossy. Stir in pecans, coconut and Kellogg's® Corn Flakes® Cereal. Drop by rounded measuring tablespoonfuls onto cookie sheets sprayed with vegetable cooking spray.

2. Bake about 15 minutes or until lightly browned. Remove immediately from cookie sheets. Cool on wire racks.

Makes about 3 dozen cookies

Variation: Fold in ½ cup crushed peppermint candy with pecans and coconut.

Crispie Treats

    4 cups miniature marshmallows
    ½ cup peanut butter
    ¼ cup margarine
    ⅛ teaspoon salt
    4 cups crisped rice cereal
1½ cups "M & M's"® Plain or Peanut Chocolate Candies

Melt together marshmallows, peanut butter, margarine and salt in large, heavy saucepan over low heat, stirring occasionally, until smooth. Pour over combined cereal and candies, tossing lightly until thoroughly coated. With greased fingers, gently shape into 1½-inch balls. Place on waxed paper; cool at room temperature until set. *Makes about 3 dozen cookies*

Variation: After cereal mixture is thoroughly coated, press lightly into greased 13×9-inch baking pan. Cool thoroughly; cut into bars. Makes about 32 bars.

Lollipop Cookies

1¼ cups granulated sugar
 1 BUTTER FLAVOR* CRISCO® Stick or 1 cup
   BUTTER FLAVOR* CRISCO® all-vegetable
   shortening
 2 eggs
¼ cup light corn syrup or regular pancake syrup
 1 tablespoon vanilla
 3 cups all-purpose flour
¾ teaspoon baking powder
½ teaspoon baking soda
½ teaspoon salt
20 flat ice cream sticks
   Colored sugars, decorative sprinkles or
   jimmies

*Butter Flavor Crisco is artificially flavored.

Lollipop Cookies

1. Combine sugar and shortening in large bowl. **Beat** at medium speed of electric mixer until well blended. **Add** eggs, syrup and vanilla. **Beat** until well blended and fluffy.

2. Combine flour, baking powder, baking soda and salt. **Add** gradually to shortening mixture at low speed. **Mix** until well blended. **Wrap** dough in plastic wrap. **Refrigerate** at least 1 hour. **Keep refrigerated** until ready to use.

3. Heat oven to 375°F. **Place** sheets of foil on countertop for cooling cookies.

4. Place colored sugar in shallow bowl. **Shape** dough into 2-inch balls. **Roll** ball in colored sugar. **Insert** wooden stick into dough ball. **Place** dough balls with sticks 3 inches apart on ungreased baking sheets. **Flatten** dough balls slightly with spatula.

5. Bake one baking sheet at a time at 375°F for 7 to 9 minutes or until just browned. *Do not overbake.* Cool 2 minutes on baking sheets. **Remove** cookies to foil to cool completely.

Makes 20 cookies

Movietime Crunch Bars

> 6 cups CAP'N CRUNCH® Cereal, Regular Flavor, divided
> 1 cup salted peanuts
> 1 cup raisins
> 1 cup semisweet chocolate chips
> 1 can (14 ounces) sweetened condensed milk

Preheat oven to 350°F. Grease 13×9-inch baking pan. Crush 4 cups cereal; spread evenly in bottom of prepared pan. Top with peanuts, raisins, chocolate chips and remaining 2 cups uncrushed cereal. Drizzle sweetened condensed milk evenly over mixture. Bake 25 to 30 minutes or until golden brown. Cool completely; cut into 2×1½-inch bars. Store tightly covered.

Makes 24 bars

OREO® Brownie Treats

> 15 OREO® Chocolate Sandwich Cookies, coarsely chopped
> 1 (21½-ounce) package deluxe fudge brownie mix, batter prepared according to package directions
> 2 pints ice cream, any flavor

Stir cookie pieces into prepared brownie batter. Grease 13×9-inch baking pan; pour batter into pan. Bake according to brownie mix package directions for time and temperature. Cool. To serve, cut into 12 squares and top each with a scoop of ice cream.

Makes 12 servings

P. B. Graham Snackers

> ½ BUTTER FLAVOR* CRISCO® Stick or ½ cup BUTTER FLAVOR* CRISCO® all-vegetable shortening
> 2 cups powdered sugar
> ¾ cup creamy peanut butter
> 1 cup graham cracker crumbs
> ½ cup semisweet chocolate chips
> ½ cup graham cracker crumbs or crushed peanuts or chocolate sprinkles (optional)

*Butter Flavor Crisco is artificially flavored.

1. Combine shortening, powdered sugar and peanut butter in large bowl. Beat at low speed of electric mixer until well blended. Stir in 1 cup crumbs and chocolate chips. Cover and refrigerate 1 hour.

2. Form dough into 1-inch balls. Roll in ½ cup crumbs. Cover and refrigerate until ready to serve.

Makes about 3 dozen cookies

Monkey Bars

   3 cups miniature marshmallows
½ cup honey
⅓ cup butter or margarine
¼ cup peanut butter
   2 teaspoons vanilla
¼ teaspoon salt
   2 cups rolled oats, uncooked
   4 cups crispy rice cereal
½ cup flaked coconut
¼ cup peanuts

Combine marshmallows, honey, butter, peanut butter, vanilla and salt in medium saucepan. Melt marshmallow mixture over low heat, stirring constantly. Combine oats, rice cereal, coconut and peanuts in 13×9-inch baking pan. Pour marshmallow mixture over dry ingredients. Mix until thoroughly coated. Press mixture firmly into pan.   *Makes 2 dozen bars*

Favorite recipe from **National Honey Board**

Old-Fashioned Ice Cream Sandwiches

   2 squares (1 ounce each) semisweet baking
        chocolate, coarsely chopped
½ cup butter or margarine, softened
½ cup sugar
   1 egg
   1 teaspoon vanilla
1½ cups all-purpose flour
¼ teaspoon baking soda
¼ teaspoon salt
     Softened vanilla ice cream

Place chocolate in 1 cup glass measuring cup. Microwave, uncovered, on HIGH 3 to 4 minutes or until chocolate is melted, stirring after 2 minutes; set aside.

Beat butter and sugar in large bowl until light and fluffy. Beat in egg and vanilla. Gradually beat in melted chocolate. Combine flour, baking soda and salt in small bowl; add to butter mixture. Form dough into two discs; wrap in plastic wrap and refrigerate until firm, at least 2 hours. (Dough may be refrigerated up to 3 days before baking.)

Preheat oven to 350°F. Grease baking sheet. Roll each piece of dough between two sheets of waxed paper to ¼- to ⅛-inch thickness. Remove top sheet of waxed paper; invert dough onto prepared baking sheet. Remove bottom sheet of waxed paper. Cut through dough with paring knife, forming 3×2-inch rectangles. Remove excess scraps of dough from edges; add to second disc of dough and repeat rolling and scoring until all of dough is cut. Prick each rectangle with fork.

Bake 10 minutes or until set. Let cookies stand on cookie sheet 1 minute. Cut through score marks with paring knife while cookies are still warm. Remove cookies to wire racks; cool completely. Spread half of cookies with softened ice cream;* top with remaining cookies.
                    Makes about 8 ice cream sandwiches

*One quart of ice cream can be softened in the microwave oven at HIGH about 20 seconds.

Old-Fashioned Ice Cream Sandwiches

Chocolate Sandwich Cookies

COOKIES
- 2 cups all-purpose flour
- ⅓ cup unsweetened cocoa powder
- 1 teaspoon baking soda
- ¼ teaspoon salt
- 6 tablespoons butter, softened
- 1 cup sugar
- 1 egg
- 1 cup milk

FILLING
- ½ cup milk
- 2 tablespoons all-purpose flour
- ½ cup butter, softened
- ½ cup sugar
- 1 teaspoon vanilla

Preheat oven to 425°F. Grease cookie sheets. For cookies, stir together 2 cups flour, cocoa, baking soda and salt in medium bowl.

Beat 6 tablespoons butter and 1 cup sugar in large bowl until fluffy. Beat in egg. Add flour mixture and 1 cup milk alternately to butter mixture, beating after each addition. Drop dough by rounded teaspoonfuls onto prepared cookie sheets. Bake about 7 minutes or until set. Remove to wire racks to cool.

For filling, stir together ½ cup milk and 2 tablespoons flour in small saucepan over low heat. Cook and stir until thick and bubbly; continue cooking 1 to 2 minutes more. Cool slightly. Beat ½ cup butter and ½ cup sugar in small bowl until fluffy. Add cooled flour mixture and vanilla. Beat until smooth. Spread filling on flat side of half the cooled cookies; top with remaining cookies.

Makes about 2½ dozen sandwich cookies

Favorite recipe from **Wisconsin Milk Marketing Board**

Brownie Sandwich Cookies

BROWNIE COOKIES
- 1 package DUNCAN HINES® Chocolate Lovers' EXXTRA Double Fudge Brownie Mix
- 1 egg
- 3 tablespoons water
- Sugar

FILLING
- 1 container (16 ounces) DUNCAN HINES® Creamy Homestyle Cream Cheese Frosting
- Red food coloring (optional)
- ½ cup semisweet mini chocolate chips

1. Preheat oven to 375°F. Grease cookie sheets.

2. For brownie cookies, combine brownie mix, fudge packet from Mix, egg and water in large bowl. Stir until well blended, about 50 strokes. Shape dough into 50 (1-inch) balls. Place 2 inches apart on prepared cookie sheets. Grease bottom of drinking glass; dip in sugar. Press gently to flatten 1 cookie to ⅜-inch thickness. Repeat with remaining cookies. Bake at 375°F for 6 to 7 minutes or until set. Cool 1 minute on cookie sheets. Remove to cooling racks. Cool completely.

3. For filling, tint frosting with red food coloring, if desired. Stir in chocolate chips.

4. To assemble, spread 1 tablespoon frosting on bottom of one cookie; top with second cookie. Press together to make sandwich cookie. Repeat with remaining cookies.

Makes 25 sandwich cookies

Brownie Sandwich Cookies

Roasted Honey Nut Sandwich Cookies

1½ cups quick oats
½ cup all-purpose flour
½ teaspoon baking powder
½ teaspoon baking soda
⅛ teaspoon salt
½ cup Roasted Honey Nut SKIPPY® Creamy
   Peanut Butter
½ cup MAZOLA® Margarine, softened
½ cup sugar
½ cup packed brown sugar
 1 egg
½ teaspoon vanilla
   Cookie Filling (recipe follows)

Preheat oven to 350°F. In medium bowl, combine oats, flour, baking powder, baking soda and salt. In large bowl, with mixer at medium speed, beat peanut butter, margarine and sugars until well blended. Beat in egg and vanilla. Stir in oat mixture until well mixed. Shape dough by heaping teaspoonfuls into balls; place 3 inches apart on ungreased cookie sheets. Flatten each ball to 2-inch round. Bake in 350°F oven 8 minutes or until golden brown. Cool 3 minutes on cookie sheets. Remove to wire racks; cool completely. Spread bottoms of half the cookies with heaping teaspoonfuls of Cookie Filling; top with remaining cookies.

Makes about 2½ dozen sandwich cookies

Cookie Filling: In small bowl, combine 1 cup Roasted Honey Nut SKIPPY® Peanut Butter and ½ cup confectioners' sugar; stir until smooth.

Chocolate Lovers' Brownie Pizza

1 package DUNCAN HINES® Chocolate Lovers'
   EXXTRA Milk Chocolate Chunk
   Brownie Mix
1 egg
⅓ cup CRISCO® Oil or CRISCO® PURITAN®
   Canola Oil
2 tablespoons water
   Strawberry slices
   Kiwifruit wedges
   Pineapple pieces
   Vanilla ice cream
   Chocolate syrup

1. Preheat oven to 350°F. Grease 13-inch round pizza pan.

2. Combine brownie mix, egg, oil and water in large bowl. Stir with spoon until well blended, about 50 strokes. Spread in pan. Bake at 350°F for 18 to 20 minutes. Cool completely.

3. Cut into wedges; decorate with assorted fruit. Top with scoops of ice cream, then drizzle with chocolate syrup.

Makes 12 servings

Tip: *For convenience, purchase precut fruit from the salad bar at your local grocery store.*

Chocolate Lovers' Brownie Pizza

Left to right: Marbled Brownies and Honey Brownies (page 117)

Marbled Brownies

Nut Cream Filling (page 117)
½ cup butter or margarine
⅓ cup HERSHEY'S Cocoa
2 eggs
1 cup sugar
1 teaspoon vanilla extract
½ cup all-purpose flour
½ teaspoon baking powder
¼ teaspoon salt

Prepare Nut Cream Filling; set aside. Preheat oven to 350°F. Grease 9-inch square baking pan.

In small saucepan, melt butter; remove from heat. Blend in cocoa; set aside to cool slightly. In medium bowl, beat eggs until foamy. Gradually add sugar and vanilla; blend well. Combine flour, baking powder and salt; blend into egg mixture. Stir in chocolate mixture. Remove ¾ cup batter; set aside. Spread remaining batter into prepared pan. Spread Nut Cream Filling over batter. Drop teaspoonfuls of reserved batter over top. Swirl gently with metal spatula or knife to marble.

Bake 35 to 40 minutes or until brownies begin to pull away from sides of pan. Cool completely on wire rack. Cut into squares. *Makes about 20 brownies*

Nut Cream Filling

    1 package (3 ounces) cream cheese, softened
    2 tablespoons butter or margarine, softened
    ¼ cup sugar
    1 egg
    ½ teaspoon vanilla extract
    ¼ to ½ teaspoon almond extract
    1 tablespoon all-purpose flour
    ¼ cup slivered almonds, toasted and chopped*

*To toast almonds, place in shallow baking pan in 350°F oven, stirring occasionally, 8 to 10 minutes or until golden brown. Cool.

In small bowl, beat cream cheese, butter and sugar until creamy. Blend in egg, vanilla and almond extract. Stir in flour and almonds.

Honey Brownies

    ½ cup sugar
    ⅓ cup butter or margarine, softened
    ⅓ cup honey
    2 teaspoons vanilla extract
    2 eggs
    ½ cup all-purpose flour
    ⅓ cup HERSHEY'S Cocoa
    ½ teaspoon salt
    ⅔ cup chopped nuts
      Creamy Brownie Frosting (recipe follows)

Preheat oven to 350°F. Grease 9-inch square baking pan. In small bowl, beat sugar and butter; blend in honey and vanilla. Add eggs; beat well. Stir together flour, cocoa and salt; gradually add to butter mixture. Stir in nuts. Spread batter into prepared pan.

Bake 25 to 30 minutes or until brownies begin to pull away from sides of pan. Cool completely in pan on wire rack; frost with Creamy Brownie Frosting, if desired. Cut into squares.
Makes about 16 brownies

Creamy Brownie Frosting

    3 tablespoons butter or margarine, softened
    3 tablespoons HERSHEY'S Cocoa
    1 tablespoon light corn syrup or honey
    ½ teaspoon vanilla extract
    1 cup powdered sugar
    1 to 2 tablespoons milk

In small bowl, beat butter, cocoa, corn syrup and vanilla. Add powdered sugar and milk; beat to spreading consistency.
Makes about 1 cup frosting

Brownie Bonanza

Orange Cappuccino Brownies

¾ cup butter
2 squares (1 ounce each) semisweet chocolate, coarsely chopped
2 squares (1 ounce each) unsweetened chocolate, coarsely chopped
1¾ cups granulated sugar
1 tablespoon instant coffee granules
3 eggs
¼ cup orange-flavored liqueur
2 teaspoons grated orange peel
1 cup all-purpose flour
1 package (12 ounces) semisweet chocolate chips
2 tablespoons shortening

Preheat oven to 350°F. Grease 13×9-inch baking pan. Melt butter and chopped chocolates in large, heavy saucepan over low heat, stirring constantly. Stir in granulated sugar and coffee granules. Remove from heat. Cool slightly. Beat in eggs, 1 at a time, with wire whisk. Whisk in liqueur and orange peel. Beat flour into chocolate mixture until just blended. Spread batter evenly in prepared pan.

Bake 25 to 30 minutes or until center is just set. Remove pan to wire rack. Meanwhile, melt chocolate chips and shortening in small, heavy saucepan over low heat, stirring constantly. Immediately, spread hot chocolate mixture over warm brownies. Cool completely in pan on wire rack. Cut into 2-inch squares. Garnish, if desired.   Makes about 2 dozen brownies

Coconut Crowned Cappuccino Brownies

6 squares (1 ounce each) semisweet chocolate, coarsely chopped
1 tablespoon freeze dried coffee granules
1 tablespoon boiling water
½ cup sugar
¼ cup butter or margarine, softened
3 eggs, divided
¾ cup all-purpose flour
½ teaspoon baking powder
¾ teaspoon ground cinnamon
¼ teaspoon salt
¼ cup whipping cream
1 teaspoon vanilla
¾ cup flaked coconut, divided
½ cup semisweet chocolate chips

Preheat oven to 350°F. Grease 8-inch square baking pan. Melt chocolate squares in small, heavy saucepan over low heat, stirring constantly; set aside. Dissolve coffee granules in boiling water in small cup; set aside. Beat sugar and butter in large bowl until light and fluffy. Beat in 2 eggs, 1 at a time. Beat in chocolate and coffee mixtures until well blended. Combine flour, baking powder, cinnamon and salt in small bowl; add to butter mixture. Beat until well blended. Spread evenly in prepared pan.

Combine whipping cream, remaining 1 egg and vanilla in medium bowl; blend well. Stir in ½ cup coconut and chocolate chips. Spread evenly over brownie batter; sprinkle with remaining ¼ cup coconut. Bake 30 to 35 minutes or until coconut is browned and center is set. Remove pan to wire rack; cool completely. Cut into 2-inch squares.

Makes about 16 brownies

Frosted Maraschino Brownies

24 red maraschino cherries, drained
1 package (23.6 ounces) brownie mix, plus ingredients to prepare mix
2 cups powdered sugar
½ cup plus 1 tablespoon butter or margarine, softened, divided
3 tablespoons milk
2 tablespoons instant vanilla pudding mix
1 ounce sweet baking chocolate

Preheat oven to temperature directed on brownie mix. Pat cherries with paper towel to remove excess juice; set aside. Prepare and bake brownie mix according to package directions in 13×9-inch baking pan; cool completely in pan on wire rack.

For frosting, beat sugar, ½ cup butter, milk and pudding mix in medium bowl until smooth. Cover; refrigerate until slightly thickened. Spread over cooled brownie in pan. Arrange cherries in rows over frosting. In small saucepan, over low heat, melt chocolate and remaining 1 tablespoon butter; stir to blend. Cool slightly. Drizzle chocolate mixture over frosting. Let chocolate set before cutting.
Makes about 24 brownies

*Favorite Recipe from **National Cherry Foundation***

Coconut Crowned Cappuccino Brownies

Cranberry Orange Ricotta Cheese Brownies

FILLING
- 1 cup ricotta cheese
- 3 tablespoons whole-berry cranberry sauce
- ¼ cup sugar
- 1 egg
- 2 tablespoons cornstarch
- ¼ to ½ teaspoon grated orange peel
- 4 drops red food color (optional)

BROWNIES
- ½ cup butter or margarine, melted
- ¾ cup sugar
- 1 teaspoon vanilla extract
- 2 eggs
- ¾ cup all-purpose flour
- ½ cup HERSHEY'₆S Cocoa
- ½ teaspoon baking powder
- ½ teaspoon salt

Preheat oven to 350°F. Grease 9-inch square baking pan.

To prepare Filling, in small bowl, beat ricotta cheese, cranberry sauce, ¼ cup sugar, 1 egg and cornstarch until smooth. Stir in orange peel and food color, if desired. Set aside.

To prepare Brownies, in another small bowl, stir together melted butter, ¾ cup sugar and vanilla; add 2 eggs, beating well. Stir together flour, cocoa, baking powder and salt; add to butter mixture, mixing thoroughly. Spread half of cocoa batter in prepared pan. Spread Filling over top. Drop remaining chocolate batter by teaspoonfuls onto Filling. Bake 40 to 45 minutes or until wooden pick inserted in center comes out clean. Cool completely in pan on wire rack. Cut into squares; refrigerate.
Makes about 16 brownies

Chocolate Almond Brownies

- 1¼ cups flour
- 2 tablespoons sugar
- ½ cup cold margarine or butter
- 1 cup chopped almonds, toasted
- 1 (14-ounce) can EAGLE® Brand Sweetened Condensed Milk (NOT evaporated milk)
- ¼ cup unsweetened cocoa powder
- 1 egg
- 2 tablespoons amaretto liqueur *or* 1 teaspoon almond extract
- ½ teaspoon baking powder
- 6 (1¼-ounce) white candy bars with almonds, broken into small pieces

Preheat oven to 350°F. In medium bowl, combine *1 cup* flour and sugar; cut in margarine with pastry blender or 2 knives, until crumbly. Add ¼ *cup* nuts. Press on bottom of ungreased 9-inch round or square baking pan. Bake 15 minutes.

In large bowl, beat sweetened condensed milk, remaining ¼ *cup* flour, cocoa, egg, amaretto and baking powder until smooth. Stir in candy pieces and ½ *cup* nuts. Spread over prepared crust. Top with remaining ¼ *cup* nuts. Bake 30 minutes or until center is set. Cool. Cut into wedges. Store tightly covered at room temperature.
Makes about 16 brownies

Prep time: 20 minutes
Bake time: 45 minutes

Cranberry Orange Ricotta Cheese Brownies

Brownie Cheesecake Bars

⅔ cup plus 2 tablespoons margarine or butter
1½ cups sugar
1½ cups flour
⅔ cup HERSHEY'S Cocoa
½ cup milk
3 eggs
3 teaspoons vanilla extract
½ teaspoon baking powder
1 cup chopped nuts, optional
1 (8-ounce) package cream cheese, softened
1 tablespoon cornstarch
1 (14-ounce) can EAGLE® Brand Sweetened
    Condensed Milk (NOT evaporated milk)

Preheat oven to 350°F. Melt ⅔ *cup* margarine. In large bowl, beat melted margarine, sugar, flour, cocoa, milk, *2 eggs, 2 teaspoons* vanilla and baking powder until well blended. Stir in nuts if desired. Spread in greased 13×9-inch baking pan.

In small bowl, beat cheese, remaining *2 tablespoons* margarine and cornstarch until fluffy. Gradually beat in sweetened condensed milk, remaining *1 egg* and *1 teaspoon* vanilla. Pour evenly over brownie batter. Bake 40 minutes or until top is lightly browned. Cool. Chill. Cut into bars. Garnish as desired. Store covered in refrigerator.   *Makes 24 to 36 bars*

Brownie Cheesecake Bars

Cheesecake Topped Brownies

1 (21.5- or 23.6-ounce) package fudge
    brownie mix
1 (8-ounce) package cream cheese, softened
2 tablespoons margarine or butter, softened
1 tablespoon cornstarch
1 (14-ounce) can EAGLE® Brand Sweetened
    Condensed Milk (NOT evaporated milk)
1 egg
1 teaspoon vanilla extract
    Ready-to-spread chocolate frosting
    (optional)

Preheat oven to 350°F. Prepare brownie mix as package directs. Spread into well-greased 13×9-inch baking pan. In small bowl, beat cream cheese, margarine and cornstarch until fluffy. Gradually beat in sweetened condensed milk, egg and vanilla until smooth. Pour evenly over brownie batter. Bake 45 minutes or until top is lightly browned. Cool. Spread with frosting if desired. Cut into squares. Store covered in refrigerator. *Makes 36 to 40 brownies*

Sour Cream Brownies

BROWNIES

1 cup water
1 cup butter
3 tablespoons unsweetened cocoa powder
2 cups all-purpose flour
2 cups granulated sugar
1 teaspoon baking soda
½ teaspoon salt
1 (8-ounce) container sour cream
2 eggs

FROSTING

4 cups sifted powdered sugar
3 tablespoons unsweetened cocoa powder
½ cup butter, softened
6 tablespoons milk
1 cup chopped nuts

For Brownies, preheat oven to 350°F. Grease 15×10×1-inch jelly-roll pan; set aside. Combine water, butter and cocoa in medium saucepan. Cook, stirring constantly, until mixture comes to a boil. Remove from heat; set aside. Combine flour, granulated sugar, baking soda and salt in medium bowl; set aside.

Beat sour cream and eggs in large bowl at medium speed of electric mixer. Gradually add hot cocoa mixture, beating well. Blend in flour mixture; beat until smooth. Pour batter into prepared pan. Bake 25 to 30 minutes or until brownie springs back when lightly touched. Cool completely in pan on wire rack.

For Frosting, combine powdered sugar and cocoa in large bowl; set aside. Beat butter in medium bowl at medium speed of electric mixer until creamy. Add powdered sugar mixture alternately with milk, beating well after each addition. Spread over cooled brownies. Sprinkle nuts over frosting. Cut into squares. *Makes about 40 brownies*

*Favorite recipe from **Wisconsin Milk Marketing Board***

Sour Cream Walnut Brownies

BROWNIES
>1 package DUNCAN HINES® Chocolate Lovers'
>   EXXTRA Brownie Mix with Walnut
>¾ cup sour cream
>1 egg
>1 teaspoon water

CHOCOLATE DRIZZLE
>½ cup semisweet chocolate chips
>2 teaspoons CRISCO® all-vegetable shortening

1. Preheat oven to 350°F. Grease 13×9-inch baking pan.

2. For brownies, combine brownie mix, sour cream, egg and water in large bowl. Stir with spoon until well blended, about 50 strokes. Spread in prepared pan. Sprinkle with walnut packet from Mix. Bake at 350°F for 25 to 28 minutes or until set.

3. For chocolate drizzle, place chocolate chips and shortening in small resealable plastic bag; seal. Place bag in bowl of hot water for several minutes. Dry with paper towel. Knead until blended and chocolate is smooth. Snip pinpoint hole in corner of bag. Drizzle chocolate over brownies. Cool completely. Cut into squares. *Makes about 24 brownies*

Marbled Fudge Nut Brownies

>2 cups (12 ounces) semisweet chocolate chips
>¼ cup margarine or butter
>2 cups biscuit baking mix
>1 (14-ounce) can EAGLE® Brand Sweetened
>   Condensed Milk (NOT evaporated milk)
>2 eggs
>1½ teaspoons vanilla extract
>1 cup chopped nuts
>1 (8-ounce) package cream cheese, softened
>⅓ cup sugar

Preheat oven to 350°F. In large saucepan, over low heat, melt *1 cup* chips with margarine. Beat in biscuit mix, sweetened condensed milk, *1 egg* and *1 teaspoon* vanilla. Stir in nuts and remaining *1 cup* chips. Reserving 1¼ cups batter, spread remainder in well-greased 13×9-inch baking pan.

In small bowl, beat cream cheese, sugar, remaining *1 egg* and *½ teaspoon* vanilla until smooth. Spread over chocolate batter. Place small spoonfuls of reserved chocolate batter over cheese mixture. With table knife or metal spatula, gently swirl through batters to marble.

Bake 30 minutes or until brownies begin to pull away from sides of pan. Cool. Cut into squares. Store covered in refrigerator. *Makes 24 to 36 brownies*

Sour Cream Walnut Brownies

Rich 'n' Creamy Brownie Bars

BROWNIES
> 1 package DUNCAN HINES® Chocolate Lovers'
> EXXTRA Double Fudge Brownie Mix
> 2 eggs
> ⅓ cup water
> ¼ cup CRISCO® Oil or CRISCO® PURITAN®
> Canola Oil
> ½ cup chopped pecans

TOPPING
> 1 package (8 ounces) cream cheese, softened
> 2 eggs
> 1 pound (3½ cups) confectioners sugar
> 1 teaspoon vanilla extract

1. Preheat oven to 350°F. Grease bottom of 13×9-inch pan.

2. For brownies, combine brownie mix, fudge packet from Mix, 2 eggs, water and oil in large bowl. Stir with spoon until well blended, about 50 strokes. Stir in pecans. Spread evenly in prepared pan.

3. For topping, beat cream cheese in large bowl at medium speed with electric mixer until smooth. Beat in 2 eggs, confectioners sugar and vanilla extract until smooth. Spread evenly over brownie mixture. Bake at 350°F for 45 to 50 minutes or until edges and top are golden brown and shiny. Cool completely in pan. Refrigerate until well chilled. Cut into bars. *Makes about 48 bars*

Bittersweet Brownies

> MAZOLA® No Stick Cooking Spray
> 4 squares (1 ounce each) unsweetened
> chocolate, melted
> 1 cup sugar
> ½ cup HELLMANN'S® or BEST FOODS® Real
> or Light Mayonnaise or Low Fat
> Cholesterol Free Mayonnaise Dressing
> 2 eggs
> 1 teaspoon vanilla
> ¾ cup flour
> ½ teaspoon baking powder
> ¼ teaspoon salt
> ½ cup chopped walnuts

Preheat oven to 350°F. Spray 8×8×2-inch baking pan with cooking spray. In large bowl, stir chocolate, sugar, mayonnaise, eggs and vanilla until smooth. Stir in flour, baking powder and salt until well blended. Stir in walnuts. Spread evenly in prepared pan.

Bake 25 to 30 minutes or until wooden pick inserted into center comes out clean. Cool in pan on wire rack. Cut into 2-inch squares. *Makes 16 brownies*

Yogurt Brownies

Yogurt Brownies

  **1 package DUNCAN HINES® Chocolate Lovers'
   Fudge Brownie Mix, Family Size
  2 egg whites
  ⅓ cup DANNON® Lowfat Vanilla Yogurt
   Confectioners sugar (optional)**

1. Preheat oven to 350°F. Grease bottom of 13×9×
2-inch pan.

2. Combine brownie mix, egg whites and yogurt in large bowl.
Stir with spoon until well blended, about 50 strokes (batter will
be thick). Spread in prepared pan. Bake at 350°F for 22 to
24 minutes or until set. Cool completely. Cut into squares.
Sprinkle with confectioners sugar, if desired.

Makes 24 brownies

Deep Dish Brownies

  **¾ cup butter or margarine, melted
  1½ cups sugar
  1½ teaspoons vanilla extract
   3 eggs
  ¾ cup all-purpose flour
  ½ cup HERSHEY₂S Cocoa
  ½ teaspoon baking powder
  ½ teaspoon salt**

Preheat oven to 350°F. Grease 8-inch square baking pan.

In medium bowl, blend butter, sugar and vanilla. Add eggs;
using spoon, beat well. Combine flour, cocoa, baking powder
and salt; gradually add to egg mixture, beating until well
blended. Spread batter into prepared pan.

Bake 40 to 45 minutes or until brownies begin to pull away from sides of pan. Cool completely in pan on wire rack. Cut into squares.   *Makes about 16 brownies*

Variation: Stir 1 cup REESE'S® Peanut Butter Chips or HERSHEY'S Semi-Sweet Chocolate Chips into batter. Proceed as above.

Chewy Chocolate Brownies

¾ cup granulated sugar
½ cup (1 stick) butter or margarine
2 tablespoons water
4 bars (8 ounces) NESTLÉ® Toll House®
    Semi-Sweet Baking Chocolate, broken up
2 eggs
2 teaspoons vanilla extract
1 cup all-purpose flour
¼ teaspoon baking soda
¼ teaspoon salt
½ cup chopped nuts (optional)

Microwave sugar, butter and water in large, microwave-safe bowl on HIGH (100%) power for 3 minutes or until mixture boils, stirring once. Add baking bars; stir until melted.

Stir in eggs, one at a time, until well blended. Stir in vanilla. Add flour, baking soda and salt; blend well. Stir in nuts. Pour into greased 13×9-inch baking pan.

Bake in preheated 350°F oven for 16 to 20 minutes or until wooden pick inserted in center comes out just slightly sticky. Cool in pan.   *Makes about 2 dozen brownies*

Saucepan method: Heat sugar, butter and water in medium saucepan just to boiling, stirring constantly. Remove from heat. Proceed as above.

Irish Brownies

4 squares (1 ounce each) semisweet baking
    chocolate, coarsely chopped
½ cup butter or margarine
½ cup sugar
2 eggs
¼ cup Irish cream liqueur
1 cup all-purpose flour
½ teaspoon baking powder
¼ teaspoon salt
    Irish Cream Frosting (recipe follows)

Preheat oven to 350°F. Grease 8-inch square baking pan. Melt chocolate and butter in medium, heavy saucepan over low heat, stirring constantly. Stir in sugar. Beat in eggs, 1 at a time, with wire whisk. Whisk in Irish cream. Add combined flour, baking powder and salt; stir until just blended. Spread batter evenly in prepared pan.

Bake 22 to 25 minutes or until center is set. Remove pan to wire rack; cool completely before frosting. Spread Irish Cream Frosting over cooled brownies. Chill at least 1 hour or until frosting is set. Cut into 2-inch squares.
Makes about 16 brownies

Irish Cream Frosting

2 ounces cream cheese (¼ cup), softened
2 tablespoons butter or margarine, softened
2 tablespoons Irish cream liqueur
1½ cups powdered sugar

Beat cream cheese and butter in small bowl with electric mixer at medium speed until smooth. Beat in Irish cream. Gradually beat in powdered sugar until smooth.
Makes about ⅔ cup frosting

Outrageous Brownies

　½ cup **MIRACLE WHIP® Salad Dressing**
　2 eggs, beaten
　¼ cup cold water
　1 (21.5-ounce) package fudge brownie mix
　3 (7-ounce) milk chocolate bars, divided
　　Walnut halves (optional)

Preheat oven to 350°F.

Mix together salad dressing, eggs and water until well blended. Stir in brownie mix, mixing just until moistened.

Coarsely chop two chocolate bars; stir into brownie mixture. Pour into greased 13×9-inch baking pan.

Bake 30 to 35 minutes or until edges begin to pull away from sides of pan. Immediately top with 1 chopped chocolate bar. Let stand about 5 minutes or until melted; spread evenly over brownies. Garnish with walnut halves, if desired. Cool. Cut into squares. *Makes about 24 brownies*

Prep Time: 10 minutes
Bake Time: 35 minutes

Best Brownies

　½ cup butter or margarine, melted
　1 cup sugar
　1 teaspoon vanilla extract
　2 eggs
　½ cup all-purpose flour
　⅓ cup **HERSHEY'S Cocoa**
　¼ teaspoon baking powder
　¼ teaspoon salt
　½ cup chopped nuts (optional)
　　Creamy Brownie Frosting (recipe follows)

Preheat oven to 350°F. Blend butter, sugar and vanilla in large bowl. Add eggs; beat well. Combine flour, cocoa, baking powder and salt; gradually blend into butter mixture. Stir in nuts.

Spread in greased 9-inch square pan. Bake for 20 to 25 minutes or until brownie begins to pull away from edges of pan. Cool; frost with Creamy Brownie Frosting. Cut into squares. *Makes about 16 brownies*

Creamy Brownie Frosting

　3 tablespoons butter or margarine, softened
　3 tablespoons **HERSHEY'S Cocoa**
　1 tablespoon light corn syrup or honey
　½ teaspoon vanilla extract
　1 cup confectioners' sugar
　1 to 2 tablespoons milk

Beat butter, cocoa, corn syrup and vanilla in small bowl. Add confectioners' sugar and milk; beat to spreading consistency.
Makes about 1 cup frosting

Chocolate Chunk Blonde Brownies

½ cup (1 stick) margarine or butter, softened
1 cup firmly packed brown sugar
1 cup granulated sugar
4 eggs
2 teaspoons vanilla
2 cups all-purpose flour
1 teaspoon CALUMET® Baking Powder
¼ teaspoon salt
1 package (8 ounces) BAKER'S® Semi-Sweet
    Chocolate, coarsely chopped
1 cup chopped nuts

Preheat oven to 350°F.

Beat margarine, sugars, eggs and vanilla until light and fluffy. Mix in flour, baking powder and salt until well blended. Stir in chocolate and nuts. Spread in greased 13×9-inch pan.

Bake for 30 minutes or until toothpick inserted into center comes out with moist crumbs. **Do not overbake.** Cool in pan; cut into squares. *Makes about 24 brownies*

Prep Time: 20 minutes
Bake Time: 30 minutes

Outrageous Brownies

ONE BOWL™ Brownies

4 squares BAKER'S® Unsweetened Chocolate
¾ cup (1½ sticks) margarine or butter
2 cups sugar
3 eggs
1 teaspoon vanilla
1 cup all-purpose flour
1 cup chopped nuts (optional)

Preheat oven to 350°F.

Microwave chocolate and margarine in large microwavable bowl on HIGH 2 minutes or until margarine is melted. **Stir until chocolate is completely melted.**

Stir sugar into melted chocolate mixture. Mix in eggs and vanilla until well blended. Stir in flour and nuts. Spread in greased 13×9-inch pan.

Bake for 30 to 35 minutes or until wooden pick inserted into center comes out with fudgy crumbs. **Do not overbake.** Cool in pan; cut into squares. *Makes about 24 brownies*

Prep time: 10 minutes
Bake time: 30 to 35 minutes

Peanut Butter Swirl Brownies: Prepare ONE BOWL™ Brownie batter as directed, reserving 1 tablespoon of the margarine and 2 tablespoons of the sugar. Add reserved ingredients to ⅔ cup peanut butter; mix well.

Place spoonfuls of peanut butter mixture over brownie batter. Swirl with knife to marbleize. Bake for 30 to 35 minutes or until wooden pick inserted into center comes out with fudgy crumbs. Cool in pan; cut into squares. Makes about 24 brownies.

Prep time: 15 minutes
Bake time: 30 to 35 minutes

Rocky Road Brownies: Prepare ONE BOWL™ Brownies as directed. Bake for 30 minutes. Sprinkle 2 cups KRAFT® Miniature Marshmallows, 1 cup BAKER'S® Semi-Sweet Real Chocolate Chips and 1 cup chopped nuts over brownies immediately. Continue baking 3 to 5 minutes or until topping begins to melt together. Cool in pan; cut into squares. Makes about 24 brownies.

Prep time: 15 minutes
Bake time: 35 minutes

Top to Bottom: Peanut Butter Swirl Brownies and Rocky Road Brownies

Brownie Fudge

  4 squares (1 ounce each) unsweetened
     chocolate
  1 cup butter or margarine
  2 cups sugar
  4 eggs
  1 cup all-purpose flour
  1 cup chopped walnuts
  2 teaspoons vanilla
     Fudge Topping (recipe follows)

Preheat oven to 350°F. Grease 13×9-inch baking pan. Melt chocolate and butter in small, heavy saucepan over low heat, stirring until completely melted; cool.

Beat sugar and eggs in large bowl with electric mixer until light and fluffy. Gradually blend chocolate mixture into egg mixture. Stir in flour, walnuts and vanilla. Spread evenly in prepared pan. Bake 25 to 35 minutes or just until set. *Do not overbake.* Meanwhile, prepare Fudge Topping. Remove brownies from oven. Immediately pour topping evenly over hot brownies. Cool in pan on wire rack. Place in freezer until firm. Cut into 1-inch squares. *Makes about 9 dozen brownies*

Fudge Topping

  4½ cups sugar
   ⅓ cup butter or margarine
    1 can (12 ounces) evaporated milk
    1 jar (7 ounces) marshmallow creme
    1 package (12 ounces) semisweet chocolate
       chips
    1 package (12 ounces) milk chocolate chips
    2 teaspoons vanilla
    2 cups walnuts, coarsely chopped

Combine sugar, butter and evaporated milk in large saucepan. Bring to a boil over medium heat; boil 5 minutes, stirring constantly. Remove from heat; add marshmallow creme, chips and vanilla. Beat with wooden spoon until smooth. Stir in walnuts.

Double Fudge Saucepan Brownies

  ½ cup sugar
   2 tablespoons butter or margarine
   2 tablespoons water
   2 cups (12-ounce package) HERSHEY'S
       Semi-Sweet Chocolate Chips, divided
   2 eggs, slightly beaten
   1 teaspoon vanilla extract
  ⅔ cup all-purpose flour
  ¼ teaspoon baking soda
  ¼ teaspoon salt
  ½ cup chopped nuts (optional)

Preheat oven to 325°F. Grease 9-inch square baking pan.

In medium saucepan, over low heat, bring sugar, butter and water to a boil, stirring constantly. Remove from heat; immediately add 1 cup of the chocolate chips, stirring until melted. Stir in eggs and vanilla until blended. Stir together flour, baking soda and salt; stir into chocolate mixture. Stir in remaining 1 cup chips and nuts, if desired. Pour batter into prepared pan.

Bake 25 to 30 minutes or until brownies begin to pull away from sides of pan. Cool completely in pan on wire rack; cut into squares. *Makes about 18 brownies*

Minted Chocolate Chip Brownies

- ¾ cup granulated sugar
- ½ cup butter or margarine
- 2 tablespoons water
- 1 cup semisweet chocolate chips or mini semisweet chocolate chips
- 1½ teaspoons vanilla
- 2 eggs
- 1¼ cups all-purpose flour
- ½ teaspoon baking soda
- ½ teaspoon salt
- 1 cup mint chocolate chips
- Powdered sugar for garnish

Preheat oven to 350°F. Grease 9-inch square baking pan. Combine sugar, butter and water in large microwavable bowl. Microwave on HIGH 2½ to 3 minutes or until butter is melted. Stir in semisweet chips; stir gently until chips are melted and mixture is well blended. Stir in vanilla; let stand 5 minutes to cool.

Beat eggs into chocolate mixture, 1 at a time. Combine flour, baking soda and salt in small bowl; add to chocolate mixture. Stir in mint chocolate chips. Spread into prepared pan.

Bake 25 minutes for fudgy brownies or 30 minutes for cakelike brownies.

Remove pan to wire rack; cool completely. Cut into 2¼-inch squares. Sprinkle with powdered sugar, if desired.

Makes about 16 brownies

Minted Chocolate Chip Brownies

Moist and Minty Brownies

1¼ cups all-purpose flour
½ teaspoon baking soda
¼ teaspoon salt
¾ cup granulated sugar
½ cup (1 stick) butter or margarine
2 tablespoons water
1½ cups (10-ounce package) NESTLÉ®
    Toll House® Mint-Chocolate Morsels,
    divided
1 teaspoon vanilla extract
2 eggs

Combine flour, baking soda and salt in small bowl. Combine sugar, butter and water in medium saucepan. Bring just to a boil, over medium heat, stirring constantly; remove from heat.* Add 1 cup morsels and vanilla; stir until smooth. Add eggs, one at a time, stirring well after each addition. Stir in flour mixture and remaining morsels.

Spread into greased 9-inch square baking pan. Bake in preheated 350°F oven for 20 to 30 minutes or until center is set. Cool (center will sink). *Makes about 16 brownies*

*Or, combine sugar, butter and water in medium microwave-safe bowl. Microwave on HIGH (100%) power for 3 minutes, stirring halfway through cooking time. Stir until smooth. Proceed as above.

Scrumptious Minted Brownies

1 package DUNCAN HINES® Chocolate Lovers'
    Fudge Brownie Mix, Family Size
1 egg
⅓ cup water
⅓ cup CRISCO® Oil or CRISCO® PURITAN®
    Canola Oil
48 chocolate crème de menthe candy wafers,
    divided

1. Preheat oven to 350°F. Grease bottom of 13×9-inch pan.

2. Combine brownie mix, egg, water and oil in large bowl. Stir with spoon until well blended, about 50 strokes. Spread in prepared pan. Bake at 350°F for 25 minutes or until set. Place 30 candy wafers evenly over hot brownies. Let stand for 1 minute to melt. Spread candy wafers to frost brownies. Score frosting into 36 bars by running tip of knife through melted candy. (Do not cut through brownies.) Cut remaining 18 candy wafers in half lengthwise; place halves on each scored bar. Cool completely. Cut into squares. *Makes 36 brownies*

Candy Dandy Brownies

BROWNIES
> 1 package DUNCAN HINES® Chocolate Lovers'
>   EXXTRA Peanut Butter Brownie Mix,
>   separated
> 1 egg
> ⅓ cup water
> ⅓ cup CRISCO® Oil or CRISCO® PURITAN®
>   Canola Oil

TOPPING
> ⅓ cup sugar
> ⅓ cup light corn syrup
>   Peanut butter packet from Mix

FROSTING
> ½ cup semisweet chocolate chips
> 2 tablespoons butter or margarine
> 1 tablespoon light corn syrup
> ¼ cup sliced almonds, for garnish

1. Preheat oven to 350°F. Grease 13×9-inch pan.

2. For Brownies, combine brownie mix, egg, water and oil in large bowl. Stir with spoon until well blended, about 50 strokes. Spread in prepared pan. Bake 25 to 28 minutes or until set. Cool in pan while preparing topping.

3. For Topping, combine sugar and ⅓ cup corn syrup in heavy saucepan. Bring to a boil on medium heat. Stir in peanut butter packet from Mix. Spread over warm brownies. Cool 10 to 15 minutes.

4. For Frosting, combine chocolate chips, butter and 1 tablespoon corn syrup in small saucepan. Cook, stirring constantly, on low heat until melted. Spread frosting over peanut butter layer. Sprinkle with almonds. Cool completely. Refrigerate until frosting is firm, about 15 minutes. Cut into squares.   *Makes about 24 brownies*

All American HEATH® Brownies

> ⅓ cup butter or margarine
> 1 square (1 ounce) unsweetened chocolate
> 1 cup sugar
> 2 eggs
> 1 teaspoon vanilla
> 1 cup all-purpose flour
> ½ teaspoon baking powder
> ¼ teaspoon salt
> 1 package (7.5 ounces) original HEATH® Bars,
>   coarsely crushed

Preheat oven to 350°F. Grease bottom of 8-inch square baking pan.

In 1½-quart saucepan, over low heat, melt butter and chocolate, stirring occasionally. Blend in sugar. Add eggs, 1 at a time, beating after each addition. Blend in vanilla. In small bowl, combine flour, baking powder and salt; add to chocolate mixture and blend. Spread batter in prepared pan.

Bake 20 minutes or until brownie starts to pull away from edge of pan. Remove from oven; sprinkle with Heath® Bars. Cover tightly with foil and cool completely on wire rack. Remove foil; cut into squares.   *Makes about 12 brownies*

Brownie Kiss Cups

Brownie Kiss Cups

1 package DUNCAN HINES® Chocolate Lovers'
Fudge Brownie Mix, Family Size
1 egg
⅓ cup water
⅓ cup CRISCO® Oil or CRISCO® PURITAN®
Canola Oil
25 milk chocolate candy kisses, unwrapped

1. Preheat oven to 350°F. Place 25 (2-inch) foil liners in muffin pans or on cookie sheets.

2. Combine brownie mix, egg, water and oil in large bowl. Stir with spoon until well blended, about 50 strokes. Fill each liner with 2 measuring tablespoonsful batter. Bake at 350°F for 17 to 20 minutes. Remove from oven. Place 1 milk chocolate candy kiss on each cupcake. Bake 1 minute longer. Cool 5 to 10 minutes in pans. Remove to cooling racks. Cool completely.

Makes 25 brownie cups

Butterscotch Brownies

1 cup butterscotch-flavored chips
¼ cup butter or margarine, softened
½ cup packed light brown sugar
2 eggs
½ teaspoon vanilla
1 cup all-purpose flour
½ teaspoon baking powder
¼ teaspoon salt
1 cup semisweet chocolate chips

Preheat oven to 350°F. Grease 9-inch square baking pan. Melt butterscotch chips in small, heavy saucepan over low heat, stirring constantly; set aside.

Beat butter and sugar in large bowl until light and fluffy. Beat in eggs, 1 at a time, beating well after each addition. Beat in vanilla and melted butterscotch chips. Combine flour, baking powder and salt in small bowl; add to butter mixture. Beat until well blended. Spread batter evenly in prepared pan.

Bake 20 to 25 minutes or until golden brown and center is set. Remove pan from oven; immediately sprinkle with chocolate chips. Let stand about 4 minutes or until chocolate is melted. Spread chocolate evenly over top. Place pan on wire rack; cool completely. Cut into 2¼-inch squares.

Makes about 16 brownies

Butterscotch Brownies

Chocolatey Rocky Road Brownies

BROWNIES
- 1 cup butter or margarine
- 4 squares (1 ounce each) unsweetened chocolate
- 1½ cups granulated sugar
- 1 cup all-purpose flour
- 3 eggs
- 1½ teaspoons vanilla
- ½ cup chopped salted peanuts

FROSTING
- ¼ cup butter or margarine
- 1 (3-ounce) package cream cheese
- 1 square (1 ounce) unsweetened chocolate
- ¼ cup milk
- 2¾ cups powdered sugar
- 1 teaspoon vanilla
- 2 cups miniature marshmallows
- 1 cup salted peanuts

Preheat oven to 350°F. Grease 13×9-inch baking pan. Set aside.

For brownies, combine 1 cup butter and 4 squares chocolate in 3-quart saucepan. Melt over medium heat, stirring constantly, 5 to 7 minutes. Add granulated sugar, flour, eggs and 1½ teaspoons vanilla; mix well. Stir in ½ cup chopped peanuts. Spread in prepared pan. Bake 20 to 25 minutes or until brownie starts to pull away from sides of pan. Cool completely.

Chocolatey Rocky Road Brownies

For frosting, combine ¼ cup butter, cream cheese, 1 square chocolate and milk in 2-quart saucepan. Melt over medium heat, stirring occasionally, 6 to 8 minutes. Remove from heat; add powdered sugar and 1 teaspoon vanilla; beat with hand mixer until smooth. Stir in marshmallows and 1 cup peanuts. Immediately spread over cooled brownies. Cool completely; cut into squares. Store refrigerated.

Makes about 4 dozen brownies

Blonde Brickle Brownies

  1⅓ cups all-purpose flour
  ½ teaspoon baking powder
  ¼ teaspoon salt
  2 eggs
  ½ cup granulated sugar
  ½ cup packed brown sugar
  ⅓ cup butter or margarine, melted
  1 teaspoon vanilla extract
  ¼ teaspoon almond extract
  1 package (7.5 ounce) BITS 'O BRICKLE®, divided
  ½ cup chopped pecans (optional)

Preheat oven to 350°F. Grease 8-inch square baking pan. Mix flour, baking powder and salt in small bowl; set aside. Beat eggs in large bowl. Gradually beat in granulated sugar and brown sugar until thick and creamy. Add melted butter, vanilla and almond extract; mix well. Gently stir in flour mixture until moistened. Fold in ⅔ cup Bits 'O Brickle® and pecans, if desired. Pour into prepared pan.

Bake 30 minutes. Remove from oven; immediately sprinkle remaining Bits 'O Brickle® over top. Cool completely in pan on wire rack. Cut into squares. *Makes about 16 brownies*

Heavenly Hash Brownies

  1 cup butter or margarine
  ¼ cup unsweetened cocoa powder
  4 eggs
  1¼ cups granulated sugar
  2 cups chopped walnuts or pecans
  1½ cups all-purpose flour
  2 teaspoons vanilla
    Creamy Cocoa Icing (recipe follows)
  1 package (10 ounces) miniature marshmallows*

*For best results, use fresh marshmallows.

Preheat oven to 350°F. Grease 13×9-inch baking pan. Melt butter in 2-quart saucepan; stir in cocoa. Remove from heat; beat in eggs and granulated sugar. Blend in nuts, flour and vanilla. Spread batter evenly in prepared pan.

Bake 20 to 25 minutes or until wooden pick inserted in center comes out clean. *Do not overbake.* Meanwhile, prepare Creamy Cocoa Icing. Remove brownies from oven. Immediately sprinkle marshmallows over hot brownies. Pour hot icing evenly over marshmallows. Cool in pan on wire rack. Cut into 2-inch squares. *Makes about 2 dozen brownies*

Creamy Cocoa Icing

  6 tablespoons butter or margarine
  ¾ cup undiluted evaporated milk
  6 cups powdered sugar
  ¾ cup unsweetened cocoa powder

Melt butter in 2-quart saucepan. Add milk, powdered sugar and cocoa. Stir over low heat until smooth and creamy.

Praline Brownies

BROWNIES
> 1 package DUNCAN HINES® Chocolate Lovers'
> EXXTRA Milk Chocolate Chunk
> Brownie Mix
> 2 eggs
> ⅓ cup water
> ⅓ cup CRISCO® Oil or CRISCO® PURITAN®
> Canola Oil
> ¾ cup chopped pecans

TOPPING
> ¾ cup firmly packed brown sugar
> ¾ cup chopped pecans
> ¼ cup butter or margarine, melted
> 2 tablespoons milk
> ½ teaspoon vanilla extract

1. Preheat oven to 350°F. Grease 9-inch square pan.

2. For brownies, combine brownie mix, eggs, water, oil and ¾ cup pecans in large bowl. Stir with spoon until well blended, about 50 strokes. Spread in prepared pan. Bake at 350°F for 35 to 40 minutes. Remove from oven.

3. For topping, combine brown sugar, ¾ cup pecans, melted butter, milk and vanilla extract in medium bowl. Stir with spoon until well blended. Spread over hot brownies. Return to oven. Bake for 15 minutes or until topping is set. Cool completely in pan on wire rack. Cut into squares.

Makes about 16 brownies

Chocolate Nut Brownies

> 1 (12-ounce) package semisweet chocolate
> chips
> ¼ cup margarine or butter
> 2 cups biscuit baking mix
> 1 (14-ounce) can EAGLE® Brand Sweetened
> Condensed Milk (NOT evaporated milk)
> 1 egg, beaten
> 1 teaspoon vanilla extract
> 1 to 1½ cups coarsely chopped walnuts
> Confectioners' sugar

Preheat oven to 350°F. In large saucepan, over low heat, melt *1 cup* chips with margarine; remove from heat. Add biscuit mix, sweetened condensed milk, egg and vanilla. Stir in nuts and remaining *1 cup* chips. Spread in well-greased 13×9-inch baking pan.

Bake 20 to 25 minutes or until brownies begin to pull away from sides of pan. Cool. Sprinkle with confectioners' sugar. Cut into squares. Store tightly covered at room temperature.

Makes 24 to 36 brownies

Fancy Walnut Brownies

BROWNIES
- 1 package DUNCAN HINES® Chocolate Lovers' EXXTRA Brownie Mix with Walnuts
- 1 egg
- ⅓ cup water
- ⅓ cup CRISCO® Oil or CRISCO® PURITAN® Canola Oil

GLAZE
- 4½ cups confectioners sugar
- ½ cup milk or water
- 24 walnut halves, for garnish

CHOCOLATE DRIZZLE
- ⅓ cup semisweet chocolate chips
- 1 tablespoon CRISCO® all-vegetable shortening

1. Preheat oven to 350°F. Place 24 (2-inch) foil liners on cookie sheets.

2. For brownies, combine brownie mix, egg, water and oil in large bowl. Stir with spoon until well blended, about 50 strokes. Stir in walnut packet from Mix. Fill each foil liner with 2 generous tablespoons batter. Bake at 350°F for 20 to 25 minutes or until set. Cool completely. Remove liners. Turn brownies upside down on cooling rack.

3. For glaze, combine confectioners sugar and milk in medium bowl. Blend until smooth. Spoon glaze over first brownie to completely cover. Top immediately with walnut half. Repeat with remaining brownies. Let glaze set. For chocolate drizzle, place chocolate chips and shortening in small resealable plastic bag; seal. Place bag in bowl of hot water for several minutes. Dry with paper towel. Knead until blended and chocolate is smooth. Cut pinpoint hole in corner of bag. Drizzle chocolate over brownies.
Makes 24 brownies

Walnut Crunch Brownies

BROWNIE LAYER
- 4 squares BAKER'S® Unsweetened Chocolate
- ¾ cup (1½ sticks) margarine or butter
- 2 cups granulated sugar
- 4 eggs
- 1 teaspoon vanilla
- 1 cup all-purpose flour

WALNUT TOPPING
- ¼ cup (½ stick) margarine or butter
- ¾ cup firmly packed brown sugar
- 2 eggs
- 2 tablespoons all-purpose flour
- 1 teaspoon vanilla
- 4 cups chopped walnuts

Preheat oven to 350°F.

Microwave unsweetened chocolate and ¾ cup margarine in large microwavable bowl on HIGH 2 minutes or until margarine is melted. **Stir until chocolate is completely melted.**

Stir granulated sugar into melted chocolate mixture. Mix in 4 eggs and 1 teaspoon vanilla until well blended. Stir in 1 cup flour. Spread in greased 13×9-inch pan.

Microwave ¼ cup margarine and brown sugar in same large bowl on HIGH 1 minute or until margarine is melted. Stir in 2 eggs, 2 tablespoons flour and 1 teaspoon vanilla until completely mixed. Stir in walnuts. Spread mixture evenly over brownie batter.

Bake for 45 minutes or until wooden pick inserted into center comes out with fudgy crumbs. **Do not overbake.** Cool in pan; cut into squares.
Makes about 24 brownies

Fancy Walnut Brownies

Peanut-Layered Brownies

BROWNIE LAYER

    4 squares BAKER'S® Unsweetened Chocolate
    ¾ cup (1½ sticks) margarine or butter
    2 cups granulated sugar
    3 eggs
    1 teaspoon vanilla
    1 cup all-purpose flour
    1 cup chopped peanuts

PEANUT BUTTER LAYER

    1 cup peanut butter
    ½ cup powdered sugar
    1 teaspoon vanilla

GLAZE

    4 squares BAKER'S® Semi-Sweet Chocolate
    ¼ cup (½ stick) margarine or butter

Preheat oven to 350°F.

Microwave unsweetened chocolate and ¾ cup margarine in large microwavable bowl on HIGH 2 minutes or until margarine is melted. **Stir until chocolate is completely melted.**

Stir granulated sugar into melted chocolate mixture. Mix in eggs and 1 teaspoon vanilla until well blended. Stir in flour and peanuts. Spread batter in greased 13×9-inch pan.

Bake for 30 to 35 minutes or until wooden pick inserted into center comes out with fudgy crumbs. **Do not overbake.** Cool in pan.

Mix peanut butter, powdered sugar and 1 teaspoon vanilla in separate bowl until well blended and smooth. Spread over brownies.

Microwave semi-sweet chocolate and ¼ cup margarine in small microwavable bowl on HIGH 2 minutes or until margarine is melted. **Stir until chocolate is completely melted.** Spread over peanut butter layer. Cool until set. Cut into squares. *Makes about 24 brownies*

Prep time: 20 minutes
Bake time: 30 to 35 minutes

Peanut Butter Paisley Brownies

    ½ cup butter or margarine, softened
    ¼ cup peanut butter
    1 cup granulated sugar
    1 cup packed light brown sugar
    3 eggs
    1 teaspoon vanilla extract
    2 cups all-purpose flour
    2 teaspoons baking powder
    ¼ teaspoon salt
    ½ cup (5.5-ounce can) HERSHEY'S Syrup

Preheat oven to 350°F. Blend butter and peanut butter in large bowl. Add granulated sugar and brown sugar; beat well. Add eggs, 1 at a time, beating well after each addition. Blend in vanilla. Combine flour, baking powder and salt; add to peanut butter mixture.

Spread half of batter in greased 13×9-inch pan. Spoon syrup over batter. Carefully spread with remaining batter. Swirl with spatula or knife to marbleize. Bake for 35 to 40 minutes or until lightly browned. Cool; cut into squares.

Makes about 36 brownies

Fudgy Bittersweet Brownie Pie

1 (12-ounce) bittersweet chocolate candy bar, broken into pieces
½ cup butter or margarine
2 eggs
½ cup sugar
1 cup all-purpose flour
½ teaspoon salt
  Vanilla ice cream
  Prepared hot fudge sauce
  Maraschino cherries (optional)

Preheat oven to 350°F. Melt chocolate and butter in small, heavy saucepan over low heat, stirring constantly. Set aside.

Beat eggs in medium bowl with electric mixer at medium speed for 30 seconds. Gradually blend in sugar; beat 1 minute. Beat in chocolate mixture, scraping down side of bowl once. Beat in flour and salt at low speed until just blended, scraping down side of bowl once. Spread batter evenly in 10-inch tart pan with removable bottom.

Bake 25 minutes or until center is just set. Remove pan to wire rack; cool completely.

To serve, cut brownie into 12 wedges. Top each piece with a scoop of vanilla ice cream. Heat fudge sauce in small microwavable bowl or glass measuring cup in microwave oven on HIGH until hot, stirring once. Spoon over ice cream; top with a cherry, if desired. *Makes 12 brownies*

Fudgy Bittersweet Brownie Pie

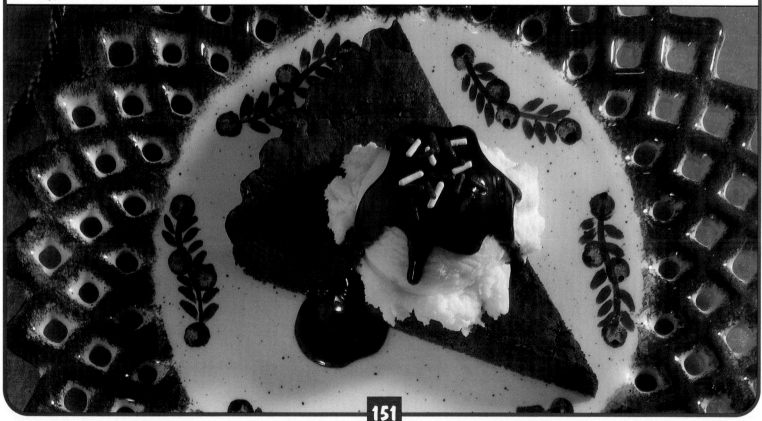

Exquisite Brownie Torte

FILLING
>   1 package (3 ounces) cream cheese, softened
>   ⅓ cup confectioners sugar
>   ¼ teaspoon almond extract
>   1 package whipped topping mix
>   ½ cup milk

RASPBERRY SAUCE
>   1 tablespoon cornstarch
>   2 tablespoons cold water
>   1 package (10 ounces) frozen raspberries in
>   light syrup, thawed
>   2 tablespoons seedless red raspberry jam
>   ¼ teaspoon lemon juice
>   1 tablespoon amaretto (optional)

>   1 package DUNCAN HINES® Chocolate Lovers'
>   EXXTRA Brownie Mix with Walnuts
>   ½ pint fresh raspberries
>   ½ cup fresh blueberries
>   Mint leaves, for garnish

1. For Filling, combine cream cheese, confectioners sugar and almond extract in large bowl. Beat at medium speed with electric mixer until blended. Add whipped topping mix and milk. Beat at high speed for 4 minutes or until mixture thickens and forms peaks. Cover. Refrigerate for 2 to 3 hours or until thoroughly chilled.

2. For Raspberry Sauce, dissolve cornstarch in water in medium saucepan. Add thawed raspberries, raspberry jam and lemon juice. Cook on medium-high heat until mixture comes to a boil. Remove from heat; add amaretto, if desired. Push mixture through sieve into small bowl to remove seeds. Refrigerate for 2 to 3 hours or until thoroughly chilled.

3. Preheat oven to 350°F. Line 9-inch springform pan with aluminum foil. Grease bottom of foil.

4. Prepare brownie batter following package directions for basic recipe. Spread in prepared pan. Bake at 350°F for 35 to 37 minutes or until set. Cool completely. Remove from pan. Peel off aluminum foil.

5. To assemble, place brownie torte on serving plate. Spread chilled Filling over top of brownie. Place ¼ cup Raspberry Sauce in small resealable plastic bag. Snip pinpoint hole in bottom corner of bag. Drizzle sauce in three concentric rings one inch apart over Filling. Draw wooden pick in straight lines from center of torte to edge through filling and sauce to form web design. Arrange fresh raspberries and blueberries in center. Garnish with mint leaves. Serve with remaining sauce.

Makes 12 to 16 servings

White Chocolate & Almond Brownies

12 ounces white chocolate, broken into pieces
1 cup unsalted butter
3 eggs
¾ cup all-purpose flour
1 teaspoon vanilla
½ cup slivered almonds

Preheat oven to 325°F. Grease and flour 9-inch square baking pan.

Melt chocolate and butter in large, heavy saucepan over low heat, stirring constantly. (White chocolate may separate.) Remove from heat when chocolate is just melted. With electric hand mixer, beat in eggs until mixture is smooth. Beat in flour and vanilla. Spread batter evenly in prepared pan. Sprinkle almonds evenly over top.

Bake 30 to 35 minutes or just until set in center. Cool completely in pan on wire rack. Cut into 2-inch squares.

Makes about 16 brownies

Left to right: Brownie Fudge (page 136) and White Chocolate & Almond Brownies

White Chocolate Brownies

**1 package DUNCAN HINES® Chocolate Lovers'
  EXXTRA Milk Chocolate Chunk
  Brownie Mix**
2 eggs
⅓ cup water
**⅓ cup CRISCO® Oil or CRISCO® PURITAN®
  Canola Oil**
¾ cup coarsely chopped white chocolate
¼ cup sliced natural almonds

1. Preheat oven to 350°F. Grease bottom of 13×9-inch baking pan.

2. Combine brownie mix, eggs, water and oil in large bowl. Stir with spoon until well blended, about 50 strokes. Stir in white chocolate. Spread in prepared pan; sprinkle with almonds. Bake at 350°F for 25 to 28 minutes or until set. Cool completely. Cut into squares.

Makes about 48 small or 24 large brownies

Tip: *For decadent brownies, combine 2 ounces coarsely chopped white chocolate and 2 teaspoons CRISCO® all-vegetable shortening in small, heavy saucepan. Melt over low heat, stirring constantly. Drizzle over brownies.*

White Chocolate Brownies

Double "Topped" Brownies

BROWNIES
- 1 package DUNCAN HINES® Chocolate Lovers'
  EXXTRA Double Fudge Brownie Mix
- 2 eggs
- 1/3 cup water
- 1/4 cup CRISCO® Oil or CRISCO® PURITAN®
  Canola Oil
- 1/2 cup flaked coconut
- 1/2 cup chopped nuts

FROSTING
- 3 cups confectioners sugar
- 1/3 cup butter or margarine, softened
- 1 1/2 teaspoons vanilla extract
- 2 to 3 tablespoons milk

TOPPING
- 3 squares (3 ounces) unsweetened chocolate
- 1 tablespoon butter or margarine

1. Preheat oven to 350°F. Grease bottom of 13×9-inch pan.

2. For brownies, combine brownie mix, fudge packet from Mix, eggs, water and oil in large bowl. Stir with spoon until well blended, about 50 strokes. Stir in coconut and nuts. Spread in prepared pan. Bake at 350°F for 27 to 30 minutes or until set. Cool completely.

3. For frosting, combine confectioners sugar, 1/3 cup butter and vanilla extract. Stir in milk, 1 tablespoon at a time, until frosting is of spreading consistency. Spread over cooled brownies. Refrigerate until frosting is firm, about 30 minutes.

4. For topping, melt chocolate and 1 tablespoon butter in small bowl over hot water; stir until smooth. Drizzle over frosting. Refrigerate until chocolate is firm, about 15 minutes. Cut into squares. *Makes about 48 brownies*

Drizzle Topped Brownies

- 1 1/4 cups all-purpose biscuit baking mix
- 1 cup sugar
- 1/2 cup HERSHEY'S Cocoa
- 1/2 cup butter or margarine, melted
- 2 eggs
- 1 teaspoon vanilla extract
- 1 cup HERSHEY'S Semi-Sweet Chocolate Chips
  or MINI CHIPS
- Quick Vanilla Glaze (recipe follows)

Heat oven to 350°F. Grease 8- or 9-inch square baking pan. In medium bowl, combine baking mix, sugar and cocoa; mix with spoon or fork until thoroughly blended. Add butter, eggs and vanilla, mixing well. Stir in chocolate chips. Spread in prepared pan.

Bake 25 to 30 minutes or until wooden pick inserted in center comes out clean. Cool completely. Drizzle Quick Vanilla Glaze over cooled brownies. Cut into squares.

Makes about 20 brownies

Quick Vanilla Glaze: In small bowl combine 1/2 cup confectioners' sugar, 1 tablespoon water and 1/4 teaspoon vanilla extract; blend well.

Simple & Sweet

Lemon Cookies

1 package **DUNCAN HINES®** Moist Deluxe Lemon Supreme Cake Mix
2 eggs
⅓ cup **CRISCO®** Oil or **CRISCO® PURITAN®** Canola Oil
1 tablespoon lemon juice
¾ cup chopped nuts or flaked coconut
Confectioners sugar

1. Preheat oven to 375°F. Grease cookie sheets.

2. Combine cake mix, eggs, oil and lemon juice in large bowl. Beat at low speed with electric mixer until well blended. Add nuts. Shape into 1-inch balls. Place on prepared cookie sheets, 1 inch apart.

3. Bake 6 to 7 minutes or until lightly browned. Cool 1 minute on cookie sheets. Remove to cooling racks. Sprinkle with confectioners sugar.

Makes about 3 dozen cookies

Tip: You can frost cookies with 1 cup confectioners sugar mixed with 1 tablespoon lemon juice instead of sprinkling cookies with confectioners sugar.

Almond Raspberry Thumbprint Cookies

1 cup butter or margarine, softened
1 cup sugar
1 can SOLO® or 1 jar BAKER® Almond Filling
2 egg yolks
1 teaspoon almond extract
2½ cups all-purpose flour
½ teaspoon baking powder
½ teaspoon salt
1 can SOLO® or 1 jar BAKER® Raspberry or Strawberry Filling

Beat butter and sugar in medium bowl with electric mixer until light and fluffy. Add almond filling, egg yolks and almond extract; beat until blended. Stir in flour, baking powder and salt with wooden spoon to make soft dough. Cover and refrigerate at least 3 hours or overnight.

Preheat oven to 350°F. Shape dough into 1-inch balls. Place 1½ inches apart on ungreased cookie sheets. Press thumb into center of each ball to make deep depression. Spoon ½ teaspoon raspberry filling into each each depression.

Bake 11 to 13 minutes or until edges of cookies are golden brown. Cool on cookie sheets 1 minute. Remove to wire racks; cool completely.   *Makes about 5 dozen cookies*

Pineapple Raisin Jumbles

2 cans (8 ounces each) DOLE® Crushed Pineapple
½ cup margarine, softened
½ cup sugar
1 teaspoon vanilla extract
1 cup all-purpose flour
4 teaspoons grated orange peel
1 cup DOLE® Blanched Slivered Almonds, toasted
1 cup DOLE® Raisins

• Preheat oven to 350°F. Drain pineapple well, pressing out excess liquid with back of spoon.

• In large bowl, beat margarine and sugar until light and fluffy. Stir in pineapple and vanilla. Beat in flour and orange peel. Stir in almonds and raisins.

• Drop heaping tablespoons of dough 2 inches apart onto greased cookie sheets.

• Bake 20 to 22 minutes or until firm. Cool on wire racks.
Makes 2 to 2½ dozen cookies

Honey Carrot Cookies

    1 cup sugar
    ½ cup margarine or butter, softened
    2 eggs
    3 tablespoons honey
    ½ teaspoon vanilla
    2¼ cups all-purpose flour
    2 teaspoons baking soda
    ½ teaspoon nutmeg
    ¼ teaspoon salt
    ½ cup shredded carrot

Preheat oven to 325°F. Combine sugar and margarine in large bowl; beat well. Add eggs, honey and vanilla; beat until well blended. Combine flour, baking soda, nutmeg and salt in medium bowl. Stir dry ingredients into butter mixture; mix well. Stir in carrot. Using well floured hands, shape dough into 1-inch balls. Place 2 inches apart on ungreased cookie sheets.

Bake 13 to 18 minutes or until edges are golden brown. Remove immediately to wire racks to cool.

Makes about 3 dozen cookies

Top to bottom: Honey Carrot Cookies and Soft Spicy Molasses Cookies (page 162)

Soft Spicy Molasses Cookies

   2 cups all-purpose flour
   1 cup sugar
   ¾ cup margarine or butter, softened
   ⅓ cup light molasses
   3 tablespoons milk
   1 egg
   ½ teaspoon baking soda
   ½ teaspoon ground ginger
   ½ teaspoon ground cinnamon
   ½ teaspoon ground cloves
   ⅛ teaspoon salt
   Sugar for rolling

Combine flour, 1 cup sugar, margarine, molasses, milk, egg, baking soda, ginger, cinnamon, cloves and salt in large bowl. Beat at low speed of electric mixer, 2 to 3 minutes. Cover; refrigerate until firm enough to handle, at least 4 hours or overnight.

Preheat oven to 350°F. Shape dough into 1-inch balls; roll in sugar. Place 2 inches apart on ungreased cookie sheets. Bake 9 to 12 minutes or until just firm to the touch. Remove immediately to wire racks to cool.

Makes about 4 dozen cookies

Honey Shortbread

   1 cup butter
   ⅓ cup honey
   1 teaspoon vanilla
   2½ cups all-purpose flour
   ¾ cup chopped pecans

Preheat oven to 300°F. Beat butter, honey and vanilla in large bowl with electric mixer at medium speed until mixture is light and fluffy. Add flour, 1 cup at a time, beating well after each addition. If dough becomes too stiff to stir, knead in remaining flour by hand. Knead in nuts. Pat dough into shortbread mold or ungreased 9-inch cast iron skillet. Score surface with knife so it can be divided into 24 wedges. With fork, prick deeply into the scores.

Bake 35 to 40 minutes. Cool in pan on wire rack 10 minutes. Remove from pan. Cut into wedges while warm.

Makes 2 dozen wedges

*Favorite recipe from **National Honey Board***

Apple Spice Cookies

   ¾ cup margarine, softened
   ¾ cup packed brown sugar
   1 egg
   1¼ cups flour
   1 cup ROMAN MEAL® Apple Cinnamon
      Multi-Bran Hot Cereal, uncooked
   ½ teaspoon baking soda
   ¼ teaspoon salt
   1 teaspoon ground cinnamon

Preheat oven to 350°F. In large bowl, beat margarine, sugar and egg. Add flour, cereal, baking soda, salt and cinnamon; mix well. Drop by rounded teaspoons onto ungreased cookie sheets. Bake 12 to 14 minutes or until golden. Cool on wire racks.

Makes about 3 dozen cookies

Honey Shortbread

Ginger Snap Oats

¾ **BUTTER FLAVOR* CRISCO®** Stick or ¾ cup **BUTTER FLAVOR* CRISCO®** all-vegetable shortening
 1 cup packed brown sugar
 ½ cup granulated sugar
 ½ cup molasses
 2 teaspoons vinegar
 2 eggs
1¼ cups all-purpose flour
 1 tablespoon ground ginger
1½ teaspoons baking soda
 ½ teaspoon ground cinnamon
 ¼ teaspoon ground cloves
2¾ cups quick oats (not instant or old-fashioned), uncooked
1½ cups raisins

*Butter Flavor Crisco is artificially flavored.

1. Heat oven to 350°F. **Grease** baking sheets with shortening. **Place** sheets of foil on countertop for cooling cookies.

2. Combine shortening, brown sugar, granulated sugar, molasses, vinegar and eggs in large mixer bowl. **Beat** at medium speed of electric mixer until well blended.

3. Combine flour, ginger, baking soda, cinnamon and cloves. **Mix** into shortening mixture at low speed until blended. **Stir** in oats and raisins.

4. Drop dough by rounded teaspoonfuls 2 inches apart onto prepared baking sheets.

Top to bottom: Ginger Snap Oats and Mom's Best Oatmeal Cookies (page 165)

5. Bake one baking sheet at a time 350°F for 11 to 14 minutes. *Do not overbake.* **Cool** 2 minutes on cookie sheets. **Remove** cookies to foil to cool completely.

Makes about 5 dozen cookies

Spicy Oatmeal Raisin Cookies

1 package **DUNCAN HINES®** Moist Deluxe
    Spice Cake Mix
4 egg whites
1 cup quick-cooking oats (not instant or
    old-fashioned), uncooked
½ cup **CRISCO®** Oil or **CRISCO® PURITAN®**
    Canola Oil
½ cup raisins

1. Preheat oven to 350°F. Grease cookie sheets.

2. Combine cake mix, egg whites, oats and oil in large mixer bowl. Beat on low speed with electric mixer until blended. Stir in raisins. Drop by rounded teaspoons onto prepared cookie sheets.

3. Bake 7 to 9 minutes or until lightly browned. Cool 1 minute on cookie sheets. Remove to cooling racks; cool completely.

Makes about 4 dozen cookies

Mom's Best Oatmeal Cookies

¾ **BUTTER FLAVOR* CRISCO®** Stick or ¾ cup
    BUTTER FLAVOR* CRISCO® all-vegetable
    shortening
1¼ cups firmly packed light brown sugar
 1 egg
⅓ cup milk
1½ teaspoons vanilla
 3 cups quick oats, uncooked
 1 cup all-purpose flour
½ teaspoon baking soda
½ teaspoon salt
¼ teaspoon ground cinnamon
 1 cup chopped pecans
⅔ cup flake coconut
⅔ cup sesame seeds

*Butter Flavor Crisco is artificially flavored.

1. Heat oven to 350°F. **Grease** baking sheets with shortening. **Place** sheets of foil on countertop for cooling cookies.

2. Combine shortening, brown sugar, egg, milk and vanilla in large mixer bowl. **Beat** at medium speed of electric mixer until well blended.

3. Combine oats, flour, baking soda, salt and cinnamon. **Mix** into shortening mixture at low speed just until blended. **Stir** in pecans, coconut and sesame seeds.

4. Drop by rounded measuring tablespoonfuls of dough 2 inches apart onto prepared baking sheets.

5. Bake one baking sheet at a time at 375°F for 10 to 12 minutes or until lightly browned. *Do not overbake.* **Cool** 2 minutes on baking sheets. **Remove** cookies to foil to cool completely.

Makes about 2½ dozen cookies

Cinnamon-Apricot Tart
Oatmeal Cookies

⅓ cup water
1 package (6 ounces) dried apricot halves, diced
¾ BUTTER FLAVOR* CRISCO® Stick or ¾ cup BUTTER FLAVOR* CRISCO® all-vegetable shortening
1¼ cups firmly packed light brown sugar
1 egg
⅓ cup milk
1½ teaspoons vanilla
3 cups quick oats, uncooked
1 cup all-purpose flour
½ teaspoon baking soda
½ teaspoon salt
¼ teaspoon cinnamon
1 cup plus 2 tablespoons chopped pecans

*Butter Flavor Crisco is artificially flavored.

1. Place ⅓ cup water in small saucepan. **Heat** to boiling over high heat. **Place** diced apricots in strainer over boiling water. **Reduce** heat to low. **Cover**; steam 15 minutes. **Set** aside.

2. Heat oven to 375°F. **Grease** baking sheets with shortening. **Place** sheets of foil on countertop for cooling cookies.

3. Combine shortening, brown sugar, egg, milk and vanilla in large bowl. **Beat** at medium speed of electric mixer until well blended.

4. Combine oats, flour, baking soda, salt and cinnamon. **Mix** into shortening mixture at low speed until just blended. **Stir** in pecans, apricots and liquid from apricots.

5. Drop by rounded measuring tablespoonfuls of dough 2 inches apart onto prepared baking sheets.

6. Bake one baking sheet at a time at 375°F for 10 to 12 minutes or until lightly browned. *Do not overbake.* **Cool** 2 minutes on baking sheets. **Remove** cookies to foil to cool completely.   *Makes 2½ dozen cookies*

Oatmeal Almond Balls

¼ cup sliced almonds
⅓ cup honey
2 egg whites
½ teaspoon ground cinnamon
⅛ teaspoon salt
1½ cups rolled oats, uncooked

Preheat oven to 350°F. Place almonds on cookie sheet; toast 8 to 10 minutes or until golden brown. Set aside. *Do not turn off oven.*

Combine honey, egg whites, cinnamon and salt in large bowl; mix well. Add oats and toasted almonds; mix well.

Drop by rounded teaspoonfuls onto ungreased nonstick cookie sheets. Bake 12 minutes or until lightly browned. Remove to wire racks to cool.   *Makes 2 dozen cookies*

Oatmeal Almond Balls

Oatmeal Lemon-Cheese Cookies

1 BUTTER FLAVOR* CRISCO® Stick or 1 cup
  BUTTER FLAVOR* CRISCO® all-vegetable
  shortening
1 package (3 ounces) cream cheese, softened
1¼ cups sugar
1 egg, separated
1 teaspoon lemon extract
2 teaspoons grated lemon peel
1¼ cups all-purpose flour
1¼ cups quick oats (not instant or
  old-fashioned), uncooked
½ teaspoon salt
1 egg
  Sugar for sprinkling
½ cup sliced almonds

*Butter Flavor Crisco is artificially flavored.

1. Heat oven to 350°F. **Place** sheets of foil on countertop for cooling cookies.

2. Combine shortening, cream cheese and sugar in large bowl. **Beat** at medium speed of electric mixer until well blended. **Beat** in egg yolk, lemon extract and lemon peel. **Combine** flour, oats and salt. **Stir** into shortening mixture with spoon until blended.

3. Drop rounded teaspoonfuls of dough 2 inches apart onto ungreased baking sheets. **Beat** whole egg with egg white. **Brush** over tops of cookies. **Sprinkle** lightly with sugar. **Press** almond slices lightly on top.

4. Bake one baking sheet at a time at 350°F for 10 to 12 minutes or until edges are lightly browned. *Do not overbake.* **Cool** 2 minutes on baking sheets. **Remove** cookies to foil to cool completely.   *Makes about 6 dozen cookies*

Old-Fashioned Oatmeal Cookies

¾ BUTTER FLAVOR* CRISCO® Stick or ¾ cup
  BUTTER FLAVOR* CRISCO® all-vegetable
  shortening
1¼ cups firmly packed brown sugar
1 egg
⅓ cup milk
1½ teaspoons vanilla
3 cups quick oats, uncooked
1 cup all-purpose flour
½ teaspoon baking soda
½ teaspoon salt
¼ teaspoon ground cinnamon
1 cup raisins
1 cup coarsely chopped walnuts

*Butter Flavor Crisco is artificially flavored.

1. Heat oven to 375°F. **Grease** baking sheets with shortening. **Place** sheets of foil on countertop for cooling cookies.

2. Combine shortening, brown sugar, egg, milk and vanilla in large bowl. **Beat** at medium speed of electric mixer until well blended.

3. Combine oats, flour, baking soda, salt and cinnamon. **Mix** into shortening mixture at low speed just until blended. **Stir** in raisins and walnuts.

4. Drop by rounded measuring tablespoonfuls of dough 2 inches apart onto prepared baking sheets.

5. Bake one baking sheet at a time at 375°F for 10 to 12 minutes or until lightly browned. *Do not overbake.* **Cool** 2 minutes on baking sheets. **Remove** cookies to foil to cool completely.   *Makes about 2½ dozen cookies*

No-Fuss Bar Cookies

No-Fuss Bar Cookies

    2 cups graham cracker crumbs (about
        24 graham cracker squares)
    1 cup semisweet chocolate chips
    1 cup flaked coconut
    ¾ cup coarsely chopped walnuts
    1 can (14 ounces) sweetened condensed milk

Preheat oven to 350°F. Grease 13×9-inch baking pan. Combine crumbs, chocolate chips, coconut and walnuts in large bowl; stir to blend. Add milk; mix until blended. Spread batter in prepared pan.

Bake 15 to 18 minutes or until edges are golden brown. Let pan stand on wire rack until completely cooled. Cut into 2¼-inch squares. *Makes about 20 cookies*

Special Treat No-Bake Squares

½ cup plus 1 teaspoon butter or margarine, divided
¼ cup granulated sugar
¼ cup unsweetened cocoa powder
1 egg
¼ teaspoon salt
1½ cups graham cracker crumbs
¾ cup flaked coconut
½ cup chopped pecans
⅓ cup butter or margarine, softened
1 package (3 ounces) cream cheese, softened
1 teaspoon vanilla
1 cup powdered sugar
1 (2-ounce) semisweet or bittersweet candy bar, broken into ½-inch pieces

Line 9-inch square pan with foil, shiny side up, allowing a 2-inch overhang on sides. Set aside.

For crust, combine ½ cup butter, granulated sugar, cocoa, egg and salt in medium saucepan. Cook over medium heat, stirring constantly, until mixture thickens, about 2 minutes. Remove from heat; stir in graham cracker crumbs, coconut and pecans. Press evenly into prepared baking pan.

For filling, beat ⅓ cup softened butter, cream cheese and vanilla in medium bowl until smooth. Gradually beat in powdered sugar. Spread over crust; refrigerate 30 minutes.

For glaze, combine candy bar and remaining 1 teaspoon butter in small resealable plastic bag; seal. Microwave at HIGH 50 seconds. Turn bag over; heat at HIGH 40 to 50 seconds or until melted. Knead bag until candy bar is smooth. Cut pinpoint hole in corner of bag; drizzle chocolate over filling. Refrigerate until firm, about 20 minutes. Remove foil from pan. Cut into 1½-inch squares.   *Makes about 25 squares*

Coconut Macaroons

2 (7-ounce) packages flaked coconut (5⅓ cups)
1 (14-ounce) can EAGLE® Brand Sweetened Condensed Milk (NOT evaporated milk)
2 teaspoons vanilla extract
1½ teaspoons almond extract

Preheat oven to 350°F. In large bowl, combine coconut, sweetened condensed milk and extracts; mix well. Drop by rounded teaspoonfuls onto aluminum foil-lined and *generously greased* cookie sheets.

Bake 8 to 10 minutes or until lightly browned around edges. *Immediately* remove from cookie sheets (macaroons will stick if allowed to cool). Store loosely covered at room temperature.
Makes about 4 dozen cookies

Variations:

Chocolate: Omit almond extract. Add 4 (1-ounce) squares unsweetened chocolate, melted. Proceed as above.

Chocolate Chip: Omit almond extract. Add 1 cup mini chocolate chips. Proceed as above.

Nutty Toppers

PEANUT BUTTER LAYER

1¼ cups firmly packed light brown sugar
¾ cup creamy peanut butter
½ CRISCO® Stick or ½ cup CRISCO®
   all-vegetable shortening
3 tablespoons milk
1 tablespoon vanilla
1 egg
1¾ cups all-purpose flour
¾ teaspoon salt
¾ teaspoon baking soda

CHOCOLATE LAYER

½ cup dough from Peanut Butter Layer
1 egg
1 tablespoon unsweetened cocoa powder
48 pecans or walnut halves

1. Heat oven to 375°F. **Place** sheets of foil on countertop for cooling cookies.

2. For Peanut Butter Layer, **combine** brown sugar, peanut butter, shortening, milk and vanilla in large bowl. **Beat** at medium speed of electric mixer until well blended. **Add** egg. **Beat** just until blended.

3. Combine flour, salt and baking soda. **Add** to shortening mixture at low speed. **Mix** just until blended.

4. For Chocolate Layer, **combine** ½ cup reserved dough from Peanut Butter Layer, egg and cocoa. **Beat** at low speed until blended.

5. Form Peanut Butter Layer dough into 1-inch balls. **Place** 2 inches apart on ungreased baking sheets. **Flatten** slightly with bottom of greased and sugared glass. **Place** leveled ½ teaspoon of Chocolate Layer on flattened dough. **Press** nut into each center. **Repeat** with remaining dough.

6. Bake one baking sheet at a time at 375°F for 7 to 8 minutes or until set and just beginning to brown. *Do not overbake.* **Cool** 2 minutes on baking sheets. **Remove** cookies to foil to cool completely.

Makes about 3 dozen cookies

Pecan Drops

¾ cup sugar
½ cup FLEISCHMANN'S® Margarine, softened
¼ cup EGG BEATERS® Real Egg Product
1 teaspoon vanilla extract
2 cups all-purpose flour
⅔ cup PLANTERS® Pecans, finely chopped
3 tablespoons jam, jelly or preserves, any
   flavor

In small bowl, with electric mixer at medium speed, beat sugar and margarine. Add egg product and vanilla; beat for 1 minute. Stir in flour until blended. Chill dough 1 hour.

Preheat oven to 350°F. Form dough into 36 (1¼-inch) balls; roll in pecans, pressing into dough. Place 2 inches apart on greased cookie sheets. Indent center of each ball with thumb or back of wooden spoon. Bake for 10 minutes; remove from oven. Spoon ¼ teaspoon jam into each cookie indentation. Bake for 2 to 5 more minutes or until lightly browned. Remove from cookie sheets; cool on wire racks.

Makes 3 dozen cookies

Left to right: Double Peanut Butter Supremes (page 179), Nutty Toppers and Oatmeal Lemon-Cheese Cookies (page 168)

Nutty Clusters

   **2 squares (1 ounce each) unsweetened
      chocolate**
   ½ cup butter or margarine, softened
   1 cup granulated sugar
   1 egg
   ⅓ cup buttermilk
   1 teaspoon vanilla
   1¾ cups all-purpose flour
   ½ teaspoon baking soda
   **1 cup mixed salted nuts, coarsely chopped
      Easy Chocolate Icing (page 175)**

Preheat oven to 400°F. Line cookie sheets with parchment paper or leave ungreased.

Melt chocolate in top of double boiler over hot, not boiling, water. Remove from heat; cool. Beat butter and granulated sugar in large bowl until smooth. Beat in egg, melted chocolate, buttermilk and vanilla until fluffy. Stir in flour, baking soda and nuts. Drop dough by teaspoonfuls 2 inches apart onto cookie sheets.

Bake 8 to 10 minutes or until slightly firm to the touch. Immediately remove cookies from cookie sheets to wire racks. Meanwhile, prepare Easy Chocolate Icing. Frost cookies while still warm.   *Makes about 4 dozen cookies*

Nutty Clusters

Easy Chocolate Icing

2 squares (1 ounce each) unsweetened
    chocolate
2 tablespoons butter or margarine
2 cups powdered sugar
2 to 3 tablespoons water

Melt chocolate and butter in small, heavy saucepan over low heat, stirring until completely melted. Add powdered sugar and water, mixing until smooth.

Orange Pecan Gems

1 package DUNCAN HINES® Moist Deluxe
    Orange Supreme Cake Mix
1 container (8 ounces) vanilla low fat yogurt
1 egg
2 tablespoons butter or margarine, softened
1 cup finely chopped pecans
1 cup pecan halves

1. Preheat oven to 350°F. Grease cookie sheets.

2. Combine cake mix, yogurt, egg, butter and chopped pecans in large bowl. Beat at low speed with electric mixer until blended. Drop by rounded teaspoonfuls 2 inches apart onto prepared cookie sheets. Press pecan half onto center of each cookie. Bake at 350°F for 11 to 13 minutes or until golden brown. Cool 1 minute on cookie sheets. Remove to cooling racks. Cool completely. Store in airtight container.

Makes about 4½ to 5 dozen cookies

Orange Pecan Gems

Chocolate-Pecan Angels

    1 cup mini semisweet chocolate chips
    1 cup chopped pecans, toasted
    1 cup sifted powdered sugar
    1 egg white

Preheat oven to 350°F. Grease cookie sheets. Combine chips, pecans and powdered sugar in medium bowl. Add egg white; mix well. Drop batter by teaspoonfuls 2 inches apart onto prepared cookie sheets.

Bake 11 to 12 minutes or until edges are light golden brown. Let cookies stand on cookie sheets 1 minute. Remove cookies to wire racks; cool completely.   *Makes about 3 dozen cookies*

Double Almond Butter Cookies

DOUGH
    2 cups butter, softened
  2½ cups powdered sugar, divided
    4 cups all-purpose flour
    2 teaspoons vanilla
FILLING
    ⅔ cup BLUE DIAMOND® Blanched Almond Paste
    ¼ cup packed light brown sugar
    ½ cup BLUE DIAMOND® Chopped Natural Almonds, toasted
    ¼ teaspoon vanilla

For Dough, beat butter and 1 cup powdered sugar. Gradually beat in flour. Beat in 2 teaspoons vanilla. Chill dough ½ hour.

For Filling, combine almond paste, brown sugar, almonds and ¼ teaspoon vanilla.

Preheat oven to 350°F. Shape dough around ½ teaspoon Filling mixture to form 1-inch balls. Place on ungreased cookie sheets.

Bake 15 minutes. Cool on wire racks. Roll cookies in remaining 1½ cups powdered sugar or sift over cookies.
Makes about 8 dozen cookies

Chocolate-Peanut Cookies

    1 cup butter or margarine, softened
    ¾ cup granulated sugar
    ¾ cup packed light brown sugar
    2 eggs
    1 teaspoon vanilla
    1 teaspoon baking soda
    ¼ teaspoon salt
  2¼ cups all-purpose flour
    2 cups chocolate-covered peanuts

Preheat oven to 375°F. Line cookie sheets with parchment paper or leave ungreased.

Beat butter, sugars, eggs and vanilla in large bowl until light and fluffy. Mix in baking soda and salt. Stir in flour to make stiff dough. Stir in chocolate-covered peanuts. Drop dough by rounded teaspoonfuls 2 inches apart onto cookie sheets.

Bake 9 to 11 minutes or until just barely golden. *Do not overbake.* Remove to wire racks to cool.
Makes about 5 dozen cookies

Peanut Meringue Cookies

4 egg whites
½ teaspoon cream of tartar
1 cup sugar
¼ cup ground peanuts

Preheat oven to 250°F. Line cookie sheets with parchment paper. Set aside.

Beat egg whites in large bowl with electric mixer until foamy. Add cream of tartar; beat until soft peaks form. Gradually add sugar; beat until stiff peaks form. Stir in peanuts.

Drop by teaspoonfuls onto prepared cookie sheets. Bake 20 minutes or until lightly browned. Cool on wire racks.

Makes about 3 dozen cookies

Chocolate Almond Buttons

1⅓ cups all-purpose flour
⅓ cup unsweetened cocoa powder
¼ teaspoon salt
1 cup BLUE DIAMOND® Blanched Almond Paste
½ cup plus 1½ tablespoons butter, softened, divided
¼ cup corn syrup
1 teaspoon vanilla extract
3 squares (1 ounce each) semisweet chocolate
⅔ cup BLUE DIAMOND® Blanched Whole Almonds, toasted

Peanut Meringue Cookies

Preheat oven to 350°F. Sift together flour, cocoa powder and salt; reserve. In large bowl, beat almond paste and ½ cup butter until smooth. Beat in corn syrup and vanilla. Beat in flour mixture until well blended. Shape dough into ¾-inch balls. Place on lightly greased cookie sheets; press down center of cookies with finger.

Bake 8 to 10 minutes or until done. (Cookies will be soft but will become firm when cooled.)

In top of double boiler, stir chocolate and remaining 1½ tablespoons butter over simmering water until melted and smooth. Using teaspoon, drizzle small amount of chocolate into center of each cookie. Press almond into chocolate on each cookie. Cool completely before removing from cookie sheets.

Makes about 6 dozen cookies

Double Peanut Butter Supremes

COOKIE
   1¼ cups firmly packed light brown sugar
    ¾ cup creamy peanut butter
    ½ CRISCO® Stick or ½ cup CRISCO®
         all-vegetable shortening
    3 tablespoons milk
    1 tablespoon vanilla
    1 egg
  1¾ cups all-purpose flour
    ¾ teaspoon salt
    ¾ teaspoon baking soda
    Granulated sugar

FILLING
   1 package (8 ounces) cream cheese, softened
   ½ cup creamy peanut butter
   ⅓ cup granulated sugar
   1 egg, slightly beaten
    Dash salt
   1 cup semisweet miniature chocolate chips

1. For Cookies, **combine** brown sugar, peanut butter, shortening, milk and vanilla in large bowl. **Beat** at medium speed of electric mixer until well blended. **Add** egg. **Beat** just until blended.

2. Combine flour and baking soda. **Add** to shortening mixture at low speed. **Mix** just until blended. **Cover** and refrigerate 1 hour.

3. Heat oven to 375°F. **Place** sheets of foil on countertop for cooling cookies.

4. For Filling, **combine** cream cheese, peanut butter, sugar, egg and salt. **Beat** at medium speed of electric mixer until blended. **Stir** in miniature chips.

5. Form dough into 1-inch balls. **Roll** in granulated sugar. **Place** 2 inches apart on ungreased baking sheets. **Press** thumb gently in center of each cookie. **Fill** center with rounded teaspoon of Filling.

6. Bake one baking sheet at a time at 375°F for 7 to 8 minutes or until set and just beginning to brown. *Do not overbake.* **Cool** 2 minutes on baking sheets. **Remove** cookies to foil to cool completely.

Makes about 3 dozen cookies

Peanut Butter Kisses

1¼ cups firmly packed light brown sugar
¾ cup creamy peanut butter
½ CRISCO® Stick or ½ cup CRISCO®
    all-vegetable shortening
3 tablespoons milk
1 tablespoon vanilla
1 egg
1¾ cups all-purpose flour
¾ teaspoon baking soda
¾ teaspoon salt
½ cup granulated sugar
48 solid milk chocolate candy drops, unwrapped

1. Heat oven to 375°F. **Place** sheets of foil on countertop for cooling cookies.

2. Combine brown sugar, peanut butter, shortening, milk and vanilla in large bowl. **Beat** at medium speed of electric mixer until well blended. **Add** egg. **Beat** just until blended.

3. Combine flour, baking soda and salt. **Add** to shortening mixture; beat at low speed until just blended.

4. Form dough into 1-inch balls. **Roll** in granulated sugar. **Place** 2 inches apart on ungreased baking sheets.

Bake one baking sheet at a time at 375°F for 6 minutes. **Press** chocolate kiss into center of each cookie. **Return** to oven. **Bake** 3 minutes. *Do not overbake.* **Cool** 2 minutes on baking sheets. **Remove** cookies to foil to cool completely.

Makes 4 dozen cookies

Easy Peanut Butter Cookies

1 (14-ounce) can EAGLE® Brand Sweetened
    Condensed Milk (NOT evaporated milk)
¾ to 1 cup peanut butter
1 egg
1 teaspoon vanilla extract
2 cups biscuit baking mix
Granulated sugar

In large bowl, beat sweetened condensed milk, peanut butter, egg and vanilla until smooth. Add biscuit mix; blend well. Chill at least 1 hour.

Preheat oven to 350°F. Shape dough into 1-inch balls. Roll in sugar. Place 2 inches apart on ungreased cookie sheets. Flatten with fork. Bake 6 to 8 minutes or until *lightly* browned (*do not overbake*). Cool. Store tightly covered at room temperature.

Makes about 5 dozen cookies

Peanut Blossoms: Shape as above. *Do not flatten.* Bake as above. Press solid milk chocolate candy drop in center of each ball immediately after baking.

Peanut Butter & Jelly Gems: Press thumb in center of each ball of dough; fill with jelly, jam or preserves. Bake as above.

Any-Way-You-Like 'em Cookies: Stir *1 cup* semisweet chocolate chips *or* chopped peanuts *or* raisins *or* flaked coconut into dough. Proceed as above.

Peanut Butter Sensations

1¼ cups firmly packed light brown sugar
¾ cup creamy peanut butter
½ CRISCO® Stick or ½ cup CRISCO®
    all-vegetable shortening
3 tablespoons milk
1 tablespoon vanilla
1 egg
1¾ cups all-purpose flour
¾ teaspoon salt
¾ teaspoon baking soda

1. Heat oven to 375°F. **Place** sheets of foil on countertop for cooling cookies.

2. Combine brown sugar, peanut butter, shortening, milk and vanilla in large bowl. **Beat** at medium speed of electric mixer until well blended. **Add** egg. **Beat** just until blended.

3. Combine flour, salt and baking soda. **Add** to shortening mixture at low speed. **Mix** just until blended.

4. Drop rounded measuring tablespoonfuls of dough 2 inches apart onto ungreased baking sheets. **Flatten** slightly in crisscross pattern with tines of fork.

3. Bake one baking sheet at a time at 375°F for 7 to 8 minutes or until set and just beginning to brown. *Do not overbake.* **Cool** 2 minutes on baking sheets. **Remove** cookies to foil to cool completely.

Makes about 3 dozen cookies

Peanut Butter Brickle Cookies

1½ cups all-purpose flour
1 cup granulated sugar
2 tablespoons packed light brown sugar
1 cup butter or margarine, softened
½ cup peanut butter
1 egg
½ teaspoon baking soda
1 teaspoon vanilla
1 package (6 ounces) almond brickle bits

Preheat oven to 350°F. Grease cookie sheets. Combine flour, granulated sugar, brown sugar, butter, peanut butter, egg, baking soda and vanilla in large bowl. Beat at medium speed of electric mixer, scraping bowl often, until well blended, 2 to 3 minutes. Stir in almond brickle bits.

Shape rounded teaspoonfuls of dough into 1-inch balls. Place 2 inches apart on prepared cookie sheets. Flatten cookies to ⅛-inch thickness with bottom of glass covered with waxed paper. Bake 7 to 9 minutes or until edges are very lightly browned.
Makes about 4 dozen cookies

Left to right: Peanut Butter Sensations, Old-Fashioned Oatmeal Cookies (page 168) and Ultimate Choclate Chip Cookies (page 14)

Peanut Butter Chewies

1 BUTTER FLAVOR* CRISCO® Stick or 1 cup BUTTER FLAVOR* CRISCO® all-vegetable shortening
1½ **cups creamy peanut butter**
1½ **cups firmly packed light brown sugar**
2 **eggs**
1 **can (14 ounces) sweetened condensed milk**
2 **teaspoons vanilla**
2 **cups all-purpose flour**
1 **teaspoon baking soda**
1 **teaspoon salt**
1½ **cups chopped pecans**

*Butter Flavor Crisco is artificially flavored.

1. Heat oven to 350°F. **Place** sheets of foil on countertop for cooling cookies.

2. Combine shortening, peanut butter and sugar in large bowl. **Beat** at medium speed of electric mixer until well blended. **Beat** in eggs, sweetened condensed milk and vanilla.

3. Combine flour, baking soda and salt. **Mix** into shortening mixture at low speed until just blended. **Stir** in pecans.

4. Drop rounded tablespoonfuls of dough 2 inches apart onto ungreased baking sheets.

5. Bake one baking sheet at a time at 350°F for 10 to 11 minutes or until lightly browned on bottom. *Do not overbake.* **Cool** 2 minutes on baking sheets. **Remove** cookies to foil to cool completely.

Makes about 4 dozen cookies

Peanut Butter Chewies

Peanut Butter Chocolate Chippers

No-Bake Peanutty Cookies

    2 cups Roasted Honey Nut SKIPPY® Creamy
        or Super Chunk® Peanut Butter
    2 cups graham cracker crumbs
    1 cup confectioners' sugar
    ½ cup KARO® Light or Dark Corn Syrup
    ¼ cup semisweet chocolate chips, melted
      Colored sprinkles (optional)

In large bowl, combine peanut butter, graham cracker crumbs, confectioners' sugar and corn syrup. Mix until smooth. Shape into 1-inch balls. Place on waxed paper-lined cookie sheets. Drizzle melted chocolate over balls; roll in colored sprinkles if desired. Store covered in refrigerator.

Makes about 5 dozen cookies

Peanut Butter Chocolate Chippers

    1 cup creamy or chunky peanut butter
    1 cup packed light brown sugar
    1 egg
    1 cup milk chocolate chips
      Granulated sugar

Preheat oven to 350°F. Combine peanut butter, brown sugar and egg in medium bowl; mix until well blended. Add chips; mix well. Roll heaping teaspoonfuls of dough into 1½-inch balls. Place balls 2 inches apart on cookie sheets. Dip fork in granulated sugar; press crisscross pattern with tines of fork on each ball, flattening to ½-inch thickness.

Bake 12 minutes or until set. Cool on cookie sheets 2 minutes. Remove cookies to wire racks; cool completely.

Makes about 2 dozen cookies

Quick Chocolate Softies

>   1 package (18.25 ounces) devil's food
>   cake mix
> 1/3 cup water
> 1/4 cup butter or margarine, softened
> 1 egg
> 1 cup white chocolate baking chips
> 1/2 cup coarsely chopped walnuts

Preheat oven to 350°F. Grease cookie sheets. Combine cake mix, water, butter and egg in large bowl. Beat with electric mixer at low speed until moistened, scraping down side of bowl once. Increase speed to medium; beat 1 minute, scraping down side of bowl once. (Dough will be thick.) Stir in chips and nuts; mix until well blended. Drop dough by heaping teaspoonfuls 2 inches apart onto prepared cookie sheets.

Bake 10 to 12 minutes or until set. Let cookies stand on cookie sheets 1 minute. Remove cookies to wire racks; cool completely.   *Makes about 4 dozen cookies*

Swiss Chocolate Crispies

>   1 package DUNCAN HINES® Moist Deluxe
>   Swiss Chocolate Cake Mix
> 1/2 cup BUTTER FLAVOR* CRISCO®
>   all-vegetable shortening
> 1/2 cup butter or margarine, softened
> 2 eggs
> 2 tablespoons water
> 3 cups crispy rice cereal, divided

*Butter Flavor Crisco is artificially flavored.

1. Combine cake mix, Butter Flavor Crisco®, butter, eggs and water in large bowl. Beat at low speed with electric mixer for 2 minutes. Fold in 1 cup cereal. Refrigerate 1 hour.

2. Crush remaining 2 cups cereal into coarse crumbs.

3. Preheat oven to 350°F. Grease cookie sheets. Shape dough into 1-inch balls. Roll in crushed cereal. Place on cookie sheets about 1 inch apart.

4. Bake 11 to 13 minutes. Cool 1 minute on cookie sheets. Remove to wire racks.   *Makes about 4 dozen cookies*

Chocolate Clouds

> 3 egg whites, at room temperature
> 1/8 teaspoon cream of tartar
> 3/4 cup sugar
> 1 teaspoon vanilla extract
> 2 tablespoons HERSHEY'S Cocoa
> 2 cups (12-ounce package) HERSHEY'S
>   Semi-Sweet Chocolate Chips

Heat oven to 300°F. Line cookie sheets with parchment paper. In large bowl, beat egg whites and cream of tartar until soft peaks form. Gradually add sugar and vanilla, beating until stiff peaks form, sugar is dissolved and mixture is glossy. Sift cocoa onto egg white mixture; gently stir just until combined. Stir in chocolate chips. Drop by heaping tablespoonfuls onto prepared cookie sheets.

Bake 35 to 40 minutes or just until dry. Carefully peel cookies off paper; cool completely on wire racks. Store covered at room temperature.   *Makes about 2 1/2 dozen cookies*

Chocolate Sugar Cookies

   3 squares BAKER'S® Unsweetened Chocolate
   1 cup (2 sticks) margarine or butter
   1 cup sugar
   1 egg
   1 teaspoon vanilla
   2 cups all-purpose flour
   1 teaspoon baking soda
   ¼ teaspoon salt
      Additional sugar

Microwave chocolate and margarine in large microwavable bowl on HIGH 2 minutes or until margarine is melted. **Stir until chocolate is completely melted.**

Stir 1 cup sugar into melted chocolate mixture until well blended. Stir in egg and vanilla until completely blended. Mix in flour, baking soda and salt. Refrigerate 30 minutes.

Heat oven to 375°F. Shape dough into 1-inch balls; roll in additional sugar. Place on ungreased cookie sheets. (If a flatter, crisper cookie is desired, flatten ball with bottom of drinking glass.)

Bake for 8 to 10 minutes or until set. Remove from cookie sheets to cool on wire racks.

Makes about 3½ dozen cookies

Prep time: 15 minutes
Chill time: 30 minutes
Bake time: 8 to 10 minutes

Jam-Filled Chocolate Sugar Cookies: Prepare Chocolate Sugar Cookie dough as directed; roll in finely chopped nuts in place of sugar. Make indentation in each ball; fill center with your favorite jam. Bake as directed.

Chocolate-Caramel Sugar Cookies: Prepare Chocolate Sugar Cookie dough as directed; roll in finely chopped nuts in place of sugar. Make indentation in each ball; bake as directed. Microwave 1 package (14 ounces) KRAFT® Caramels with 2 tablespoons milk in microwavable bowl on HIGH 3 minutes or until melted, stirring after 2 minutes. Fill centers of cookies with caramel mixture. To drizzle with chocolate, place 1 square BAKER'S® Semi-Sweet Chocolate in resealable plastic bag. Close bag tightly. Microwave on HIGH about 1 minute or until chocolate is melted. Fold down top of bag; cut pinpoint hole in bottom corner. Holding top of bag tightly, drizzle chocolate through opening over cookies.

Chocolate Chip Macaroons

   2½ cups flaked coconut
      ⅔ cup mini semisweet chocolate chips
      ⅔ cup sweetened condensed milk
       1 teaspoon vanilla

Preheat oven to 350°F. Grease cookie sheets. Combine coconut, chocolate chips, milk and vanilla in medium bowl; mix until well blended. Drop dough by rounded teaspoonfuls 2 inches apart onto prepared cookie sheets. Press dough gently with back of spoon to flatten slightly.

Bake 10 to 12 minutes or until light golden brown. Let cookies stand on cookie sheets 1 minute. Remove cookies to wire racks; cool completely.

Makes about 3½ dozen cookies

Top to bottom: Chocolate Sugar Cookies, Jam-Filled Chocolate Sugar Cookies and Chocolate-Caramel Sugar Cookies

Chocolate-Orange Chip Cookies

½ **BUTTER FLAVOR* CRISCO® Stick** or ½ **cup BUTTER FLAVOR* CRISCO® all-vegetable shortening**
1¼ cups packed brown sugar
2 squares (1 ounce each) unsweetened chocolate, melted and cooled
1 egg
2 tablespoons orange juice concentrate
2 tablespoons grated orange peel
1 teaspoon vanilla
1½ cups all-purpose flour
¾ teaspoon baking soda
¼ teaspoon salt
1 cup semisweet chocolate chips
½ cup blanched slivered almonds

*Butter Flavor Crisco is artificially flavored.

1. Heat oven to 375°F. **Place** sheets of foil on countertop for cooling cookies.

2. Combine shortening, brown sugar and melted chocolate in large bowl. **Beat** at medium speed of electric mixer until well blended. **Beat** in egg, orange juice, orange peel and vanilla.

3. Combine flour, baking soda and salt. **Mix** into shortening mixture at low speed until well blended. **Stir** in chocolate chips and nuts.

Top to bottom: Chocolate-Orange Chip Cookies and Cinnamon-Apricot Tart Oatmeal Cookies (page 166)

4. Drop tablespoonfuls of dough 2 inches apart onto ungreased baking sheets.

5. Bake one baking sheet at a time at 375°F for 7 to 9 minutes or until set. *Do not overbake.* **Cool** 2 minutes on baking sheets. **Remove** cookies to foil to cool completely.

Makes about 3½ dozen cookies

HERSHEY®S Vanilla Chip Chocolate Cookies

  1 cup (2 sticks) butter or margarine, softened
  2 cups sugar
  2 eggs
  2 teaspoons vanilla extract
  2 cups all-purpose flour
  ¾ cup HERSHEY®S Cocoa
  1 teaspoon baking soda
  ½ teaspoon salt
  1⅔ cups (10-ounce package) HERSHEY®S Vanilla
    Milk Chips

Heat oven to 350°F. In large bowl, beat butter and sugar until creamy. Add eggs and vanilla extract; beat until light and fluffy. Stir together flour, cocoa, baking soda and salt; gradually blend into butter mixture. Stir in vanilla milk chips. Drop by rounded teaspoonfuls onto ungreased cookie sheets.

Bake 8 to 9 minutes. (Do not overbake, cookies will be soft. They will puff while baking; flatten upon cooling.) Cool slightly; remove from cookie sheets to wire racks. Cool completely.

Makes about 4½ dozen cookies

HERSHEY®S Vanilla Chip Chocolate Cookies

Fudgy Walnut Cookie Wedges

1 (20-ounce) package refrigerated cookie dough, any flavor
1 (12-ounce) package HERSHEY®S Semi-Sweet Chocolate Chips
2 tablespoons margarine or butter
1 (14-ounce) can EAGLE® Brand Sweetened Condensed Milk (NOT evaporated milk)
1 teaspoon vanilla extract
½ cup chopped walnuts

Preheat oven to 350°F. Divide cookie dough into thirds. With floured hands, press on bottom of 3 aluminum foil-lined 9-inch round cake pans *or* press into 9-inch circles on ungreased cookie sheets. Bake 10 to 20 minutes or until golden. Cool.

In heavy saucepan over medium heat, melt chips and margarine with sweetened condensed milk. Cook and stir until thickened, about 5 minutes; add vanilla. Spread over cookie circles. Top with walnuts. Chill. Cut into wedges. Store loosely covered at room temperature. *Makes about 36 wedges*

Fudgy Raisin Pixies

½ cup butter
2 cups granulated sugar
4 eggs
2 cups all-purpose flour, divided
¾ cup unsweetened cocoa powder
2 teaspoons baking powder
½ teaspoon salt
½ cup chocolate-covered raisins
Powdered sugar

Beat butter and sugar in large bowl until light and fluffy. Add eggs; mix until well blended. Combine 1 cup flour, cocoa, baking powder and salt in small bowl; add to butter mixture. Mix until well blended. Stir in remaining 1 cup flour and chocolate-covered raisins. Cover; refrigerate until firm, 2 hours or overnight.

Preheat oven to 350°F. Grease cookie sheets. Coat hands with powdered sugar. Shape rounded teaspoonfuls of dough into 1-inch balls; roll in powdered sugar. Place 2 inches apart on prepared cookie sheets. Bake 14 to 17 minutes or until firm to the touch. Remove immediately from cookie sheets; cool completely on wire racks. *Makes about 4 dozen cookies*

Devil's Food Fudge Cookies

1 package DUNCAN HINES® Moist Deluxe Devil's Food Cake Mix
2 eggs
½ cup CRISCO® Oil or CRISCO® PURITAN® Canola Oil
1 cup semisweet chocolate chips
½ cup chopped walnuts

1. Preheat oven to 350°F. Grease baking sheets.

2. Combine cake mix, eggs and oil in large bowl. Stir until thoroughly blended. Stir in chocolate chips and walnuts. (Mixture will be stiff.) Shape dough into 36 (1¼-inch) balls. Place 2 inches apart on prepared baking sheets.

3. Bake at 350°F for 10 to 11 minutes. (Cookies will look moist.) *Do not overbake.* Cool 2 minutes on baking sheets. Remove to cooling racks. Cool completely. Store in airtight container. *Makes 3 dozen cookies*

Almond Fudge Topped Shortbread

- **1 cup margarine or butter, softened**
- **½ cup confectioners' sugar**
- **¼ teaspoon salt**
- **1¼ cups unsifted flour**
- **1 (12-ounce) package HERSHEY'S Semi-Sweet Chocolate Chips**
- **1 (14-ounce) can EAGLE® Brand Sweetened Condensed Milk (NOT evaporated milk)**
- **½ teaspoon almond extract**
- **Sliced almonds, toasted**

Preheat oven to 350°F. In large bowl, beat margarine, sugar and salt until fluffy. Add flour; mix well. With floured hands, press evenly into greased 13×9-inch baking pan. Bake 20 to 25 minutes or until lightly browned.

In heavy saucepan, over low heat, melt chips and sweetened condensed milk, stirring constantly. Remove from heat; stir in extract. Spread evenly over baked shortbread. Garnish with almonds; press down firmly. Cool. Chill 3 hours or until firm. Cut into bars. Store covered at room temperature.

Makes 24 to 36 bars

Almond Fudge Topped Shortbread

Marshmallow Sandwich Cookies

⅔ cup butter or margarine, softened
1¼ cups sugar
¼ cup light corn syrup
1 egg
1 teaspoon vanilla
2 cups all-purpose flour
½ cup unsweetened cocoa powder
2 teaspoons baking soda
¼ teaspoon salt
Sugar for rolling
24 large marshmallows

Preheat oven to 350°F. Beat butter and 1¼ cups sugar in large bowl until light and fluffy. Beat in corn syrup, egg and vanilla. Combine flour, cocoa, baking soda and salt in medium bowl; add to butter mixture. Beat until well blended. Cover and refrigerate dough 15 minutes or until firm enough to roll into balls.

Place sugar in shallow dish. Roll tablespoonfuls of dough into 1-inch balls; roll in sugar to coat. Place 3 inches apart on ungreased cookie sheets. Bake 10 to 11 minutes or until set. Remove cookies to wire rack; cool completely.

To assemble sandwiches, place one marshmallow on flat side of one cookie on paper plate. Microwave at HIGH 12 seconds or until marshmallow just begins to melt. Immediately place another cookie, flat side down, on top of warm marshmallow; press together slightly.

Makes about 2 dozen sandwich cookies

Cocoa Snickerdoodles

1 cup butter or margarine, softened
¾ cup packed brown sugar
¾ cup plus 2 tablespoons granulated sugar, divided
2 eggs
2 cups uncooked rolled oats
1½ cups all-purpose flour
¼ cup plus 2 tablespoons unsweetened cocoa powder, divided
1 teaspoon baking soda
2 tablespoons ground cinnamon

Preheat oven to 375°F. Lightly grease cookie sheets or line with parchment paper.

Beat butter, brown sugar and ¾ cup granulated sugar in large bowl until light and fluffy. Add eggs; mix well. Combine oats, flour, ¼ cup cocoa and baking soda in medium bowl. Stir into butter mixture until blended.

Mix remaining 2 tablespoons granulated sugar, remaining 2 tablespoons cocoa and cinnamon in small bowl. Drop dough by rounded teaspoonfuls into cinnamon mixture; toss to coat. Place 2 inches apart on prepared cookie sheets.

Bake 8 to 10 minutes or until firm in center. *Do not overbake.* Remove to wire racks to cool.

Makes about 4½ dozen cookies

Elegant Treasures

Almond Rice Madeleines

1 cup whole blanched
  almonds, lightly
  toasted
¾ cup flaked coconut
1½ cups sugar
  3 cups cooked rice, chilled
  3 egg whites
  Fresh raspberries
  Frozen nondairy whipped
  topping (optional)

Preheat oven to 350°F. Spray madeleine pans* with nonstick cooking spray. Place almonds in blender or food processor; process until finely ground. Add coconut and sugar to processor; process until coconut is finely minced. Add rice; pulse to blend. Add egg whites; pulse to blend. Spoon mixture evenly into prepared madeleine pans, filling to tops.

Bake 25 to 30 minutes or until lightly browned. Cool completely in pans on wire racks. Cover and refrigerate 2 hours or until ready to serve. Run sharp knife around each shell; gently remove from pan. Invert onto serving plates. Serve with raspberries and whipped topping, if desired.   Makes about 3 dozen cookies

*Substitute miniature muffin tins for madeleine pans, if desired.

Favorite recipe from **USA Rice Council**

Chocolate Madeleines

1¼ cups all-purpose flour
1 cup sugar
⅛ teaspoon salt
¾ cup butter, melted (no substitutes)
⅓ cup HERSHEY₍S Cocoa
3 eggs
2 egg yolks
½ teaspoon vanilla extract
Chocolate Frosting (recipe follows)

Preheat oven to 350°F. Lightly grease indentations of madeleine mold pan (each shell is 3×2 inches). In medium saucepan, stir together flour, sugar and salt. Combine melted butter and cocoa; stir into dry ingredients. In small bowl, lightly beat eggs, egg yolks and vanilla with fork until well blended; stir into chocolate mixture, blending well. Cook over very low heat, stirring constantly, until mixture is warm. *Do not simmer or boil.* Remove from heat. Fill each mold half full with batter (do not overfill).

Bake 8 to 10 minutes or until wooden toothpick inserted in center comes out clean. Invert onto wire rack; cool completely. Prepare Cocoa Frosting; frost flat sides of cookies. Press frosted sides together, forming shells.

Makes about 1½ dozen filled cookies

Chocolate Frosting

1¼ cups powdered sugar
2 tablespoons HERSHEY₍S Cocoa
2 tablespoons butter, softened (no substitutes)
2 to 2½ tablespoons milk
½ teaspoon vanilla extract

In small bowl, stir together powdered sugar and cocoa. In separate small bowl, beat butter and ¼ cup of the cocoa mixture until fluffy. Gradually add remaining cocoa mixture alternately with milk, beating to spreading consistency. Stir in vanilla.

Brandy Lace Cookies

¼ cup sugar
¼ cup MAZOLA® Margarine
¼ cup KARO® Light or Dark Corn Syrup
½ cup all-purpose flour
¼ cup very finely chopped pecans or walnuts
2 tablespoons brandy
Melted white and/or semisweet chocolate (optional)

Preheat oven to 350°F. Lightly grease and flour cookie sheets.

In small saucepan, combine sugar, margarine and corn syrup. Bring to a boil over medium heat, stirring constantly. Remove from heat. Stir in flour, pecans and brandy. Drop 12 half teaspoonfuls of batter 2 inches apart onto prepared cookie sheets.

Bake 6 minutes or until golden. Cool 1 to 2 minutes or until cookies can be lifted but are still warm and soft. Remove cookies with spatula. Curl cookies around handle of wooden spoon; slide off when crisp. If cookies harden before curling, return to oven to soften. If desired, drizzle with melted chocolate. *Makes 4 to 5 dozen cookies*

Top to bottom: Brandy Lace Cookies and Kentucky Bourbon Pecan Tarts (page 208)

Chocolate Lace Cornucopias

½ cup firmly packed brown sugar
½ cup corn syrup
¼ cup (½ stick) margarine or butter
4 squares BAKER'S® Semi-Sweet Chocolate
1 cup all-purpose flour
1 cup finely chopped nuts
    Whipped cream or COOL WHIP® Whipped
      Topping, thawed

Preheat oven to 350°F.

Microwave sugar, corn syrup and margarine in large microwavable bowl on HIGH 2 minutes or until boiling. Stir in chocolate until completely melted. Gradually stir in flour and nuts until well blended.

Drop by level tablespoonfuls, 4 inches apart, onto foil-lined cookie sheets. Bake 10 minutes. Lift foil and cookies onto wire racks. Cool on wire racks 3 to 4 minutes or until cookies can be easily peeled off foil. Remove foil. Cover wire racks with paper toweling. Finish cooling cookies on covered wire racks.

Place several cookies, lacy side down, on foil-lined cookie sheets. Heat at 350°F for 2 to 3 minutes or until slightly softened. Remove from foil, one at a time, and roll, lacy side out, to form cones. Cool completely. Just before serving, fill with whipped cream.   *Makes about 30 cornucopias*

Prep time: 20 minutes
Bake time: 12 to 13 minutes

Saucepan preparation: Mix sugar, corn syrup and margarine in 2-quart saucepan. Bring to a boil over medium heat, stirring constantly. Remove from heat; stir in chocolate until melted. Continue as above.

Chocolate-Gilded Danish Sugar Cones

½ cup butter or margarine, softened
½ cup sugar
½ cup all-purpose flour
2 egg whites
1 teaspoon vanilla
3 ounces bittersweet chocolate *or* ½ cup
    semisweet chocolate chips

Preheat oven to 400°F. Generously grease 4 cookie sheets. Beat butter and sugar in large bowl until light and fluffy. Blend in flour. In clean, dry bowl, beat egg whites until foamy; blend into butter mixture. Add vanilla. Using teaspoon, place 4 mounds of dough 4 inches apart on each prepared cookie sheet. Spread mounds with small spatula dipped in water to 3-inch diameter.

Bake 1 sheet at a time, 5 to 6 minutes or until edges are just barely golden. (Do not overbake or cookies become crisp too quickly and are difficult to shape.) Remove from oven and quickly loosen each cookie from cookie sheet with thin spatula. Shape each cookie into a cone. Cookies will become firm as they cool. If cookies become too firm to shape, return to oven for a few seconds to soften.

Melt chocolate in small bowl over hot water. Stir until smooth. When all cookies are baked and cooled, dip wide ends into melted chocolate; let stand until chocolate is set.
          Makes about 16 cookies

Chocolate-Gilded Danish Sugar Cones

Pecan Florentines

¾ **cup pecan halves, pulverized***
½ **cup all-purpose flour**
⅓ **cup packed brown sugar**
¼ **cup light corn syrup**
¼ **cup butter or margarine**
 2 **tablespoons milk**
⅓ **cup semisweet chocolate chips**

*To pulverize pecans, place in food processor or blender. Process until thoroughly ground with a dry, not pasty, texture.

Preheat oven to 350°F. Line cookie sheets with foil; lightly grease foil. Combine pecans and flour in small bowl. Combine sugar, syrup, butter and milk in medium saucepan. Stir over medium heat until mixture comes to a boil. Remove from heat; stir in flour mixture.

Drop batter by teaspoonfuls about 3 inches apart onto prepared cookie sheets. Bake 10 to 12 minutes or until lacy and golden brown (cookies are soft when hot, but become crispy as they cool). Cool completely on foil.

Place chocolate chips in small resealable plastic bag; close securely. Set bag in bowl of hot water until chips are melted, being careful not to let any water into bag. Remove bag from water. Knead bag lightly to check that chips are completely melted. Pat bag dry. With scissors, cut pinpoint hole in corner from one side of bag. Squeeze melted chocolate over cookies to decorate. Let stand until chocolate is set. Peel cookies off foil.   *Makes about 3 dozen cookies*

Caramel Lace Chocolate Chip Cookies

¼ **BUTTER FLAVOR* CRISCO® Stick** or ¼ **cup BUTTER FLAVOR* CRISCO® all-vegetable shortening**
½ **cup light corn syrup**
 1 **tablespoon brown sugar**
½ **teaspoon vanilla**
1½ **teaspoons grated orange peel (optional)**
½ **cup all-purpose flour**
¼ **teaspoon salt**
⅓ **cup semisweet chocolate chips**
⅓ **cup coarsely chopped pecans**

*Butter Flavor Crisco is artificially flavored.

1. Heat oven to 375°F. **Grease** baking sheets with shortening. **Place** foil on countertop for cooling cookies.

2. Combine shortening, corn syrup, brown sugar, vanilla and orange peel in large bowl. **Beat** at medium speed of electric mixer until well blended. **Combine** flour and salt. **Mix** into shortening mixture at low speed until blended. **Stir** in chocolate chips and nuts. **Drop** teaspoonfuls of dough 4 inches apart onto baking sheets.

3. Bake one baking sheet at a time at 375°F for 5 minutes or until edges are golden brown. (Chips and nuts will remain in center while dough spreads out.) *Do not overbake.* **Cool** 2 minutes on baking sheets. **Lift** each cookie edge with spatula. **Grasp** cookie edge gently and lightly pinch or flute the edge, bringing it up to chips and nuts in center. **Work** around each cookie until completely fluted. **Remove** cookies to foil to cool completely.   *Makes about 3 dozen cookies*

Left to right: Double-Dipped Hazelnut Crisps (page 204) and Pecan Florentines

Double-Dipped Hazelnut Crisps

¾ **cup semisweet chocolate chips**
1¼ **cups all-purpose flour**
¾ **cup powdered sugar**
⅔ **cup whole hazelnuts, toasted, hulled and pulverized***
¼ **teaspoon instant espresso powder**
   Dash salt
½ **cup butter or margarine, softened**
2 **teaspoons vanilla**
4 **squares (1 ounce each) bittersweet or semisweet chocolate**
2 **teaspoons shortening, divided**
4 **ounces white chocolate**

*To pulverize hazelnuts, place in food processor or blender. Process until thoroughly ground with a dry, not pasty, texture.

Preheat oven to 350°F. Lightly grease cookie sheets or line with parchment paper. Melt chocolate chips in top of double boiler over hot, not boiling, water. Remove from heat; cool. Blend flour, sugar, hazelnuts, espresso powder and salt in large bowl. Blend in butter, melted chocolate and vanilla until dough is stiff but smooth. (If dough is too soft to handle, cover and refrigerate until firm.)

Roll out dough, ¼ at a time, to ⅛-inch thickness on lightly floured surface. Cut out with 2-inch scalloped round cutters. Place 2 inches apart on prepared cookie sheets. Bake 8 minutes or until not quite firm. (Cookies should not brown. They will puff up during baking and then fall again.) Remove to wire racks to cool.

Place bittersweet chocolate and 1 teaspoon shortening in small bowl. Place bowl over hot water; stir until chocolate is melted and smooth. Dip cookies, 1 at a time, halfway into bittersweet chocolate. Place on waxed paper; refrigerate until chocolate is set. Repeat melting process with white chocolate and remaining 1 teaspoon shortening. Dip other halves of cookies into white chocolate; refrigerate until set. Store cookies in airtight container in cool place. (If cookies are frozen, chocolate may discolor.)   *Makes about 4 dozen cookies*

Double-Dipped Chocolate Peanut Butter Cookies

½ **cup butter or margarine, softened**
½ **cup plus 2 tablespoons granulated sugar, divided**
½ **cup packed light brown sugar**
½ **cup chunky or creamy peanut butter**
1 **egg**
1 **teaspoon vanilla**
1¼ **cups all-purpose flour**
½ **teaspoon baking powder**
½ **teaspoon baking soda**
½ **teaspoon salt**
1½ **cups semisweet chocolate chips**
3 **teaspoons shortening, divided**
1½ **cups milk chocolate chips**

Preheat oven to 350°F. Beat butter, ½ cup granulated sugar and brown sugar in large bowl until light and fluffy. Beat in peanut butter, egg and vanilla. Combine flour, baking powder, baking soda and salt in small bowl. Gradually add to butter mixture; mix well. Roll heaping tablespoonfuls of dough into 1½-inch balls. Place balls 2 inches apart on ungreased cookie sheets. (If dough is too soft to roll into balls, refrigerate 30 minutes.)

Dip fork into remaining 2 tablespoons granulated sugar; press crisscross indentation on each ball, flattening to ½-inch thickness. Bake 12 minutes or until set. Let cookies stand on cookie sheets 2 minutes. Remove cookies to wire rack; cool completely.

Melt semisweet chocolate chips and 1½ teaspoons shortening in top of double boiler over hot, not boiling, water. Dip one third of each cookie into semisweet chocolate; place on waxed paper. Let stand until chocolate is set, about 30 minutes.

Melt milk chocolate chips with remaining 1½ teaspoons shortening in top of double boiler over hot, not boiling, water. Dip opposite one third of each cookie into milk chocolate; place on waxed paper. Let stand until chocolate is set, about 30 minutes. *Makes about 2 dozen cookies*

Double-Dipped Chocolate Peanut Butter Cookies

Chocolate-Dipped Brandy Snaps

½ cup (1 stick) butter
½ cup granulated sugar
⅓ cup dark corn syrup
½ teaspoon ground cinnamon
¼ teaspoon ground ginger
1 cup all-purpose flour
2 teaspoons brandy
1 cup (6-ounces) NESTLÉ® Toll House®
    Semi-Sweet Chocolate Morsels
1 tablespoon shortening
⅓ cup finely chopped nuts

Melt butter, sugar, corn syrup, cinnamon and ginger in medium, heavy saucepan over low heat, stirring until smooth. Remove from heat; stir in flour and brandy. Drop six rounded teaspoons of batter onto ungreased baking sheet about 3 inches apart.

Bake in preheated 300°F oven for 10 to 14 minutes or until deep caramel color. Let stand for a few seconds. Remove from baking sheet and immediately roll around wooden spoon handle; cool.

Microwave morsels and shortening in medium, microwave-safe bowl on HIGH (100%) power for 45 seconds; stir. Microwave at additional 10 to 20 second intervals, stirring until smooth. Dip cookies halfway in melted chocolate; shake off excess. Sprinkle with nuts; set on waxed paper-lined baking sheets. Chill for 10 minutes or until chocolate is set. Store in airtight container in refrigerator.

Makes about 3 dozen cookies

Cherry Surprises

1 package DUNCAN HINES® Golden Sugar
    Cookie Mix
48 to 54 candied cherries
¾ cup semisweet chocolate chips
1½ teaspoons CRISCO® all-vegetable shortening

1. Preheat oven to 375°F. Grease cookie sheets.

2. Prepare cookie mix following package directions for cut cookies. Shape thin layer of dough around each candied cherry. Place 2 inches apart on prepared cookie sheets. Bake at 375°F for 8 minutes or until set but not browned. Cool 1 minute on cookie sheets. Remove to cooling racks. Cool completely.

3. Combine chocolate chips and shortening in small resealable plastic bag. Place bag in bowl of hot water for several minutes. Dry with paper towel. Knead until blended and chocolate is smooth. Cut pinpoint hole in corner of bag. Drizzle chocolate over cooled cookies. Allow drizzle to set before storing between layers of waxed paper in airtight container.

Makes 4 to 4½ dozen cookies

Kentucky Bourbon Pecan Tarts

    Cream Cheese Pastry (recipe follows)
 2 eggs
 ½ cup granulated sugar
 ½ cup KARO® Light or Dark Corn Syrup
 2 tablespoons bourbon
 1 tablespoon MAZOLA® Margarine, melted
 ½ teaspoon vanilla
 1 cup chopped pecans
    Confectioners' sugar (optional)

Preheat oven to 350°F. Prepare Cream Cheese Pastry. Divide dough in half; set aside 1 half. On floured surface, roll out pastry to ⅛-inch thickness. *If necessary, add small amount of flour to keep pastry from sticking.* Cut into 12 (2¼-inch) rounds. Press evenly into bottoms and up sides of 1¾-inch muffin pan cups. Repeat with remaining pastry. Refrigerate.

In medium bowl, beat eggs slightly. Stir in granulated sugar, corn syrup, bourbon, margarine and vanilla until well blended. Spoon 1 heaping teaspoon pecans into each pastry-lined cup; top with 1 tablespoon corn syrup mixture.

Bake 20 to 25 minutes or until lightly browned and toothpick inserted into center comes out clean. Cool in pans 5 minutes. Remove; cool completely on wire rack. If desired, sprinkle cookies with confectioners' sugar.   *Makes 2 dozen cookies*

Prep Time: 45 minutes
Bake Time: 25 minutes plus cooling

Cream Cheese Pastry

 1 cup all-purpose flour
 ¾ teaspoon baking powder
    Pinch salt
 ½ cup MAZOLA® Margarine, softened
 1 package (3 ounces) cream cheese, softened
 2 teaspoons sugar

In small bowl, combine flour, baking powder and salt. In large bowl, mix margarine, cream cheese and sugar until well combined. Stir in flour mixture until well blended. Press firmly into ball with hands.

No-Bake Cherry Crisps

 ¼ cup butter or margarine, softened
 1 cup powdered sugar
 1 cup peanut butter
 ¼ cup plus 2 tablespoons mini semisweet chocolate chips
 ¼ cup chopped pecans
 1⅓ cups crisp rice cereal
 ½ cup maraschino cherries, drained, dried and chopped
 1 to 2 cups flaked coconut for rolling

In large bowl, beat butter, sugar and peanut butter. Stir in chips, pecans, cereal and cherries. Mix well. Shape teaspoonfuls of dough into 1-inch balls. Roll in coconut. Place on cookie sheets and chill in refrigerator 1 hour. Store in refrigerator.   *Makes about 3 dozen cookies*

Chocolate Chip Cordials

COOKIES
- 1 package DUNCAN HINES® Chocolate Chip Cookie Mix
- 1 egg
- ⅓ cup CRISCO® Oil or CRISCO® PURITAN® Canola Oil
- 3 tablespoons water
- 1⅓ cups chopped pecans
- ⅓ cup chopped red candied cherries
- ⅓ cup flaked coconut
- Pecan or cherry halves for garnish

CHOCOLATE GLAZE
- 1½ squares (1½ ounces) semisweet chocolate
- 3 tablespoons butter or margarine

1. Preheat oven to 375°F. Place 1¾-inch paper liners in 42 mini muffin cups.

2. For cookies, combine cookie mix, egg, oil and water in large bowl. Stir until thoroughly blended. Stir in chopped pecans, chopped cherries and coconut. Fill cups with cookie dough. Top with pecan or cherry halves. Bake at 375°F for 13 to 15 minutes or until light golden brown. Cool completely.

3. For chocolate glaze, melt chocolate and butter in small bowl over hot water. Stir until smooth. Drizzle over cordials. Refrigerate until chocolate is firm. Store in airtight container.

Makes 42 cordials

Chocolate Chip Cordials

Choco-Caramel Delights

½ cup butter or margarine, softened
⅔ cup sugar
1 egg, separated
2 tablespoons milk
1 teaspoon vanilla extract
1 cup all-purpose flour
⅓ cup HERSHEY₅'S Cocoa
¼ teaspoon salt
1 cup finely chopped pecans
  Caramel Filling (page 211)
½ cup HERSHEY₅'S Semi-Sweet Chocolate Chips
      or Premium Semi-Sweet Chocolate Chunks
1 teaspoon shortening

In medium bowl, beat butter, sugar, egg yolk, milk and vanilla until blended. Stir together flour, cocoa and salt; blend into butter mixture. Refrigerate dough at least 1 hour or until firm enough to handle.

Preheat oven to 350°F. Beat egg white slightly. Shape dough into 1-inch balls. Dip each ball into egg white; roll in pecans to coat. Place on lightly greased cookie sheets. Press thumb gently in center of each ball. Bake 10 to 12 minutes or until set. While cookies are baking, prepare Caramel Filling. Remove cookies from oven; press center of each cookie again with thumb to make indentation. Immediately spoon about ½ teaspoon Caramel Filling in center of each cookie. Carefully remove from cookie sheets; cool on wire racks.

Choco-Caramel Delights

In small microwave-safe bowl, place chocolate chips and shortening. Microwave at HIGH (100%) 1 minute or until softened; stir. Allow to stand several minutes to finish melting; stir until smooth. Place waxed paper under wire racks with cookies. Drizzle chocolate mixture over tops of cookies.

Makes about 2 dozen cookies

Caramel Filling: In small saucepan, combine 14 unwrapped light caramels and 3 tablespoons whipping cream. Cook over low heat, stirring frequently, until caramels are melted and mixture is smooth.

Jam-Up Oatmeal Cookies

1 BUTTER FLAVOR* CRISCO® Stick or 1 cup
    BUTTER FLAVOR* CRISCO® all-vegetable
    shortening
1½ cups firmly packed brown sugar
2 eggs
2 teaspoons almond extract
2 cups all-purpose flour
1 teaspoon baking powder
1 teaspoon salt
½ teaspoon baking soda
2½ cups quick oats (not instant or
    old-fashioned), uncooked
1 cup finely chopped pecans
1 jar (12 ounces) strawberry jam
  Sugar for sprinkling

*Butter Flavor Crisco is artificially flavored.

1. Combine shortening and brown sugar in large bowl. **Beat** at medium speed of electric mixer until well blended. **Beat** in eggs and almond extract.

2. Combine flour, baking powder, salt and baking soda. **Mix** into shortening mixture at low speed until just blended. **Stir** in oats and chopped nuts with spoon. **Cover** and refrigerate at least 1 hour.

3. Heat oven to 350°F. Grease baking sheets with shortening. **Place** sheets of foil on countertop for cooling cookies.

4. Roll out dough, half at a time, to about ¼-inch thickness on floured surface. **Cut** out with 2½-inch round cookie cutter. **Place** 1 teaspoonful of jam in center of half of the rounds. **Top** with remaining rounds. **Press** edges to seal. **Prick** centers with wooden pick or fork; sprinkle with sugar. **Place** 1 inch apart on cookie sheets.

5. Bake one baking sheet at a time at 350°F for 12 to 15 minutes or until lightly browned. *Do not overbake.* **Cool** 2 minutes on baking sheets. **Remove** cookies to foil to cool completely.

Makes about 2 dozen cookies

Black and White Cut-Outs

  1 cup butter or margarine, softened
  ¾ cup granulated sugar
  ¾ cup packed light brown sugar
  2 eggs
  1 teaspoon vanilla
  2¾ cups plus 2 tablespoons all-purpose flour,
      divided
  1 teaspoon baking soda
  ¾ teaspoon salt
  ¼ cup unsweetened cocoa powder
  1 (4-ounce) white baking bar, broken into
      ½-inch pieces
  1 (4-ounce package) semisweet chocolate chips
  Assorted decorative candies (optional)

Beat butter, granulated sugar and brown sugar in large bowl until light and fluffy. Beat in eggs, 1 at a time. Beat in vanilla. Combine 2¾ cups flour, baking soda and salt in medium bowl; add to butter mixture. Beat until well blended. Remove half of dough from bowl; reserve. To make chocolate dough, beat cocoa into remaining dough with spoon until well blended. To make butter cookie dough, beat remaining 2 tablespoons flour into reserved dough. Flatten each half of dough into a disc; wrap in plastic wrap and refrigerate about 1½ hours or until firm. (Dough may be refrigerated up to 3 days before baking).

Preheat oven to 375°F. Working with one type of dough at a time, place dough on lightly floured surface. Roll out dough to ¼-inch thickness. Cut dough into desired shapes with cookie cutters. Place cookies 1 inch apart on ungreased cookie sheets. Bake 9 to 11 minutes or until set. Let cookies stand on cookie sheets 2 minutes. Remove cookies to wire racks; cool completely.

For white chocolate drizzle, place baking bar pieces in small resealable plastic bag; seal bag. Heat in microwave oven at MEDIUM 2 minutes. Turn bag over; heat at MEDIUM 2 to 3 minutes or until melted. Knead bag until baking bar is smooth. Cut pinpoint hole in corner of bag; pipe or drizzle melted chocolate onto chocolate cookies. Decorate as desired with assorted candies. Let stand until white chocolate is set, about 30 minutes.

For chocolate drizzle, place chocolate chips in small resealable plastic bag; seal bag. Heat in microwave oven at HIGH 1 minute. Turn bag over; heat at HIGH 1 to 2 minutes or until chocolate is melted. Knead bag until chocolate is smooth. Cut pinpoint hole in corner of bag; pipe or drizzle chocolate onto butter cookies. Decorate as desired with assorted candies. Let stand until chocolate is set, about 40 minutes.

Makes 3 to 4 dozen cookies

Black and White Sandwiches: Cut cookies out with cookie cutter. Bake according to above directions. Spread thin layer of prepared frosting on bottom side of chocolate cookie. Place bottom side of butter cookie over frosting. Drizzle either side of cookie with melted chocolate or white chocolate.

Almond Hearts

    1 package **DUNCAN HINES**® **Golden Sugar Cookie Mix**
    ¾ cup ground almonds
    2 egg yolks
    ⅓ cup **CRISCO**® Oil or **CRISCO**® **PURITAN**® Canola Oil
    1½ tablespoons water
    14 ounces (6 cubes) vanilla flavored candy coating
    Pink candy coating, for garnish

1. Preheat oven to 375°F.

2. Combine cookie mix, ground almonds, egg yolks, oil and water in large bowl. Stir until thoroughly blended.

3. Divide dough in half. Roll half the dough between 2 sheets of waxed paper into 11-inch circle. Slide onto flat surface. Refrigerate about 15 minutes. Repeat with remaining dough. Loosen top sheet of waxed paper from dough. Turn over and remove second sheet of waxed paper. Cut dough with 2½-inch heart cookie cutter. Place cut-outs 2 inches apart on ungreased cookie sheets. (Roll leftover cookie dough to ⅛-inch thickness between sheets of waxed paper. Chill before cutting.) Repeat cutting with remaining dough circle. Bake at 375°F for 6 to 8 minutes or until light golden brown. Cool 1 minute on cookie sheets. Remove to cooling racks. Cool completely.

Almond Hearts

4. Place vanilla candy coating in 1-quart saucepan on low heat; stir until melted and smooth. Dip half of one heart cookie into candy coating. Allow excess to drip back into pan. Place cookie on waxed paper. Repeat with remaining cookies. Place pink candy coating in small saucepan on low heat. Stir until melted and smooth. Pour into pastry bag fitted with small writing tip. Decorate tops of cookies as desired.

Makes about 5 dozen cookies

Peanut Butter Cut-Out Cookies

½ cup butter or margarine
1 cup REESE'S® Peanut Butter Chips
⅔ cup packed light brown sugar
1 egg
¾ teaspoon vanilla extract
1⅓ cups all-purpose flour
¾ teaspoon baking soda
½ cup finely chopped pecans
Chocolate Chip Glaze (recipe follows)

In medium saucepan, place butter and peanut butter chips; cook over low heat, stirring constantly, until melted. Pour into large bowl; add brown sugar, egg and vanilla, beating until well blended. Stir in flour, baking soda and pecans, blending well. Refrigerate 15 to 20 minutes or until firm enough to roll.

Preheat oven to 350°F. Roll a small portion of dough at a time on lightly floured board, or between 2 pieces of waxed paper to ¼-inch thickness. (Keep remaining dough in refrigerator.) With cookie cutters, cut dough into desired shapes; place on ungreased cookie sheets. Bake 7 to 8 minutes or until almost set (do not overbake). Cool 1 minute; remove from cookie sheets to wire racks. Cool completely. Drizzle Chocolate Chip Glaze onto each cookie; allow to set.

Makes about 3 dozen cookies

Chocolate Chip Glaze: In top of double boiler over hot, not boiling, water melt 1 cup HERSHEY'S Semi-Sweet Chocolate Chips with 1 tablespoon shortening; stir until smooth. Remove from heat; cool slightly, stirring occasionally.

Chocolate Chip Almond Biscotti

2¾ cups all-purpose flour
1½ teaspoons baking powder
¼ teaspoon salt
½ cup butter or margarine, softened
1 cup sugar
3 eggs
3 tablespoons almond-flavored liqueur
1 tablespoon water
1 cup mini semisweet chocolate chips
1 cup sliced almonds, toasted, chopped

Combine flour, baking powder and salt in medium bowl. Beat butter and sugar in large bowl with electric mixer at medium speed until light and fluffy. Beat in eggs, 1 at a time, beating well after each addition. Add liqueur and water. Gradually add flour mixture. Stir in chips and almonds.

Divide dough into fourths. Shape each quarter into a 15-inch log. Wrap securely. Refrigerate about 2 hours or until firm.

Preheat oven to 375°F. Lightly grease cookie sheet. Place each log on prepared cookie sheet. With floured hands, shape each log 2 inches wide and ½ inch thick.

Bake 15 minutes. Remove logs from oven to cutting surface. Cut each log with serrated knife into 1-inch diagonal slices. Return slices, cut side up, to cookie sheets; bake 7 minutes. Turn cookies over; bake 7 minutes or until cut surfaces are golden brown and cookies are dry. Cool completely.

Makes 4 dozen cookies

Viennese Meringue Bars

　1 cup butter or margarine, softened
1¼ cups sugar, divided
　2 egg yolks
　¼ teaspoon salt
2¼ cups all-purpose flour
　1 cup seedless raspberry jam
1½ cups mini semisweet chocolate chips
　3 egg whites
　½ cup slivered almonds, toasted

Preheat oven to 350°F. Beat butter and ½ cup sugar in large bowl with electric mixer at medium speed until light and fluffy. Beat in egg yolks and salt. Gradually add flour. Beat at low speed until well blended.

With buttered fingers, pat dough evenly into ungreased 15×10-inch jelly-roll pan. Bake 22 to 25 minutes or until light golden brown. Remove from oven; immediately spread jam over crust. Sprinkle evenly with chocolate chips.

For meringue topping, beat egg whites in clean, large bowl with electric mixer on high speed until foamy. Gradually beat in remaining ¾ cup sugar until stiff peaks form. Gently stir in almonds with rubber spatula.

Spoon meringue over chocolate chips; spread evenly with small spatula. Bake 20 to 25 minutes or until golden brown. Cool completely on wire rack. Cut into bars.

Makes about 2 dozen bars

Chocolate Pecan Pie Bars

CRUST
1½ cups all-purpose flour
　½ cup (1 stick) butter, softened
　¼ cup packed brown sugar
FILLING
　3 eggs
　¾ cup dark or light corn syrup
　¾ cup granulated sugar
　2 tablespoons (¼ stick) butter, melted
　1 teaspoon vanilla extract
1½ cups coarsely chopped pecans
　2 cups (12-ounce package) NESTLÉ® Toll
　　　House® Semi-Sweet Chocolate Morsels

For Crust, beat flour, butter and brown sugar in small bowl until crumbly. Press into greased 13×9-inch baking pan. Bake in preheated 350°F oven for 12 to 15 minutes or until lightly browned.

For Filling, beat eggs, corn syrup, granulated sugar, melted butter and vanilla in medium bowl with wire whisk. Stir in pecans and morsels. Pour evenly over baked crust. Bake in preheated 350°F oven for 25 to 30 minutes or until set. Cool. Cut into bars.

Makes 3 dozen bars

Raspberry Fudge Brownies

½ cup butter or margarine
3 squares (1 ounce each) bittersweet
   chocolate*
2 eggs
1 cup sugar
1 teaspoon vanilla
¾ cup all-purpose flour
¼ teaspoon baking powder
   Dash salt
½ cup sliced or slivered almonds
½ cup raspberry preserves
1 cup (6 ounces) milk chocolate chips

*Bittersweet chocolate is available in specialty food stores. One square unsweetened chocolate plus two squares semisweet chocolate may be substituted.

Preheat oven to 350°F. Grease and flour 8-inch square baking pan.

Melt butter and bittersweet chocolate in small, heavy saucepan over low heat. Remove from heat; cool. Beat eggs, sugar and vanilla in large bowl until light. Beat in chocolate mixture. Stir in flour, baking powder and salt until just blended. Spread ¾ of batter in prepared pan; sprinkle almonds over top.

Bake 10 minutes. Remove from oven; spread preserves over almonds. Carefully spoon remaining batter over preserves, smoothing top. Bake 25 to 30 minutes or just until top feels firm.

Remove from oven; sprinkle chocolate chips over top. Let stand a few minutes until chips melt, then spread evenly over brownies. Cool completely in pan on wire rack. When chocolate is set, cut into 2-inch squares.   *Makes 16 brownies*

Pinwheel Cookies

½ cup BUTTER FLAVOR* CRISCO® all-vegetable
   shortening
⅓ cup plus 1 tablespoon butter, softened and
   divided
2 egg yolks
½ teaspoon vanilla
1 package DUNCAN HINES® Moist Deluxe
   Fudge Marble Cake Mix

*Butter Flavor Crisco is artificially flavored.

1. Combine Butter Flavor Crisco®, ⅓ cup butter, egg yolks and vanilla in large bowl. Mix at low speed of electric mixer until blended. Set aside cocoa packet from cake mix. Gradually add cake mix. Blend well.

2. Divide dough in half. Add cocoa packet and remaining 1 tablespoon butter to one half of dough. Knead until well blended and chocolate colored.

3. Roll out yellow dough between two pieces of waxed paper into 18×12×⅛-inch rectangle. Repeat for chocolate dough. Remove top pieces of waxed paper from chocolate and yellow dough. Lay yellow dough directly on top of chocolate. Remove remaining layers of waxed paper. Roll up jelly-roll fashion, beginning at wide side. Refrigerate 2 hours.

4. Preheat oven to 350°F. Grease cookie sheets.

5. Cut dough into ⅛-inch slices. Place sliced dough 1 inch apart on prepared cookie sheets. Bake 9 to 11 minutes or until lightly browned. Cool 5 minutes on cookie sheets. Remove to cooling racks.   *Makes about 3½ dozen cookies*

Raspberry Fudge Brownies

Cinnamon Nut Chocolate Spirals

1½ cups all-purpose flour
¼ teaspoon salt
⅓ cup butter or margarine, softened
¾ cup sugar, divided
1 egg
1 cup mini semisweet chocolate chips
1 cup very finely chopped walnuts
2 teaspoons ground cinnamon
3 tablespoons butter or margarine, melted

Combine flour and salt in small bowl; set aside. Beat softened butter and ½ cup sugar in large bowl with electric mixer at medium speed until light and fluffy. Beat in egg. Gradually add flour mixture. Dough will be stiff. (If necessary, knead dough by hand until it holds together.)

Roll out dough between 2 sheets of waxed paper into 12×10-inch rectangle. Remove waxed paper from top of rectangle.

Combine chips, walnuts, remaining ¼ cup sugar and cinnamon in medium bowl. Pour hot melted butter over chocolate chip mixture; mix well.(Chips will partially melt.) Spoon mixture over dough. Spread evenly, leaving ½-inch border on long edges.

Using bottom sheet of waxed paper as a guide and starting at long side, tightly roll up dough jelly-roll style, removing waxed paper as you roll. Wrap in plastic wrap; refrigerate 30 minutes to 1 hour.*

Preheat oven to 350°F. Lightly grease cookie sheets. Unwrap dough. Using heavy thread or dental floss, cut dough into ½-inch slices. Place slices 2 inches apart on prepared cookie sheets.

Bake 14 minutes or until edges are light golden brown. Cool completely on wire racks.   *Makes about 2 dozen cookies*

*If dough is chilled longer than 1 hour, slice with a sharp, thin knife.

Chocolate Pistachio Fingers

¾ cup butter or margarine, softened
⅓ cup sugar
⅓ cup (about 3 ounces) almond paste
1 egg yolk
1⅔ cups all-purpose flour
1 cup (6 ounces) semisweet chocolate chips
½ cup finely chopped natural pistachios

Preheat oven to 350°F. Line cookie sheets with parchment paper or lightly grease and dust with flour. Beat butter and sugar in large bowl until blended. Add almond paste and egg yolk; beat until light. Blend in flour to make a smooth dough. (If dough is too soft to handle, cover and refrigerate until firm.) Turn out onto lightly floured board. Divide dough into 8 equal pieces; divide each piece in half. Roll each half into 12-inch rope; cut each rope into 2-inch lengths. Place 2 inches apart on prepared cookie sheets.

Bake 10 to 12 minutes or until edges just begin to brown. Remove to wire racks to cool. Melt chocolate chips in small bowl over hot water. Stir until smooth. Dip both ends of cookies about ½ inch into melted chocolate, then dip chocolate ends into pistachios. Place on waxed paper; let stand until chocolate is set.   *Makes 8 dozen cookies*

Cinnamon Nut Chocolate Spirals

Left to right: Chocolate Spritz (page 224), Orange & Chocolate Ribbon Cookies (page 223), Chocolate Cherry Cookies (page 223), Chocolate Pistachio Fingers (page 220) and Mocha Pecan Pinwheels

Mocha Pecan Pinwheels

  1 square (1 ounce) unsweetened chocolate
½ cup (1 stick) butter or margarine, softened
¾ cup packed brown sugar
  1 egg
  1 teaspoon vanilla
¼ teaspoon baking soda
1¾ cups all-purpose flour
½ cup chopped pecans
  1 teaspoon instant espresso coffee powder

Melt chocolate in small bowl over hot, not boiling, water. Stir until smooth. Beat butter, brown sugar, egg, vanilla and baking soda in large bowl, blending well. Stir in flour to make stiff dough. Remove half of dough; place in another bowl. Blend pecans and coffee powder into half of dough. Stir melted chocolate into remaining half of dough. Cover both halves of dough; refrigerate 30 minutes.

Roll out light-colored dough to 15×8-inch rectangle between 2 sheets of plastic wrap. Roll chocolate dough out to same dimensions between 2 more sheets of plastic wrap. Remove top sheets of plastic wrap. Place light-colored dough on top of chocolate dough. Remove remaining sheets of plastic wrap. Roll up firmly, jelly-roll fashion, starting with long side. Wrap in plastic; freeze until firm enough to handle. (Dough can be frozen up to 6 weeks.)

Preheat oven to 350°F. Line cookie sheets with parchment paper or leave ungreased. Cut frozen dough into ¼-inch-thick slices; place 2 inches apart on prepared cookie sheets. Bake 9 to 12 minutes or until set. Remove to wire racks to cool.

Makes about 5 dozen cookies

Orange & Chocolate Ribbon Cookies

    1 cup butter or margarine, softened
    ½ cup sugar
    3 egg yolks
    2 teaspoons grated orange peel
    1 teaspoon orange extract
    2¼ cups all-purpose flour, divided
    3 tablespoons unsweetened cocoa powder
    1 teaspoon vanilla
    1 teaspoon chocolate extract

Beat butter, sugar and egg yolks in large bowl until light and fluffy. Remove half of mixture; place in another bowl. Add orange peel, orange extract and 1¼ cups of the flour to one half of mixture; mix until blended and smooth. Shape into a ball. Add cocoa, vanilla and chocolate extract to second half of mixture; beat until smooth. Stir in remaining 1 cup flour; mix until blended and smooth. Shape into a ball. Cover both halves of dough; refrigerate 10 minutes.

Roll out each dough separately on lightly floured surface to 12×4-inch rectangle. Pat edges of dough to straighten; use rolling pin to level off thickness. Place one dough on top of the other. Using sharp knife, make lengthwise cut through center of doughs. Lift half of dough onto other to make long, 4-layer strip of dough. With hands, press dough strips together. Wrap in plastic wrap; refrigerate at least 1 hour or up to 3 days. (For longer storage, freeze up to 6 weeks.)

Preheat oven to 350°F. Lightly grease cookie sheets or line with parchment paper. Cut dough crosswise into ¼-inch-thick slices; place 2 inches apart on prepared cookie sheets. Bake 10 to 12 minutes or until very lightly browned. Remove to wire racks to cool.

Makes about 5 dozen cookies

Chocolate Cherry Cookies

    2 squares (1 ounce each) unsweetened
        chocolate
    ½ cup butter or margarine, softened
    ½ cup sugar
    1 egg
    2 cups cake flour
    1 teaspoon vanilla
    ¼ teaspoon salt
        Maraschino cherries, well drained (about 48)
    1 cup (6 ounces) semisweet or milk chocolate
        chips

Melt unsweetened chocolate in top of double boiler over hot, not boiling, water. Remove from heat; cool. Beat butter and sugar in large bowl until light. Add egg and melted chocolate; beat until fluffy. Stir in cake flour, vanilla and salt until well blended. Cover; refrigerate until firm, about 1 hour. Preheat oven to 400°F. Lightly grease cookie sheets or line with parchment paper. Shape dough into 1-inch balls. Place 2 inches apart on prepared cookie sheets. With knuckle of finger, make deep indentation in center of each ball. Place cherry into each indentation. Bake 8 minutes or just until set. Meanwhile, melt chocolate chips in small bowl over hot water. Stir until melted. Remove cookies to wire racks. Drizzle melted chocolate over tops of cookies while still warm. Refrigerate until chocolate is set.

Makes about 4 dozen cookies

Two-Toned Spritz Cookies

1 square (1 ounce) unsweetened chocolate,
   coarsely chopped
1 cup butter or margarine, softened
1 cup sugar
1 egg
1 teaspoon vanilla
2¼ cups all-purpose flour
¼ teaspoon salt

Melt chocolate in small, heavy saucepan over low heat, stirring constantly; set aside. Beat butter and sugar in large bowl until light and fluffy. Beat in egg and vanilla. Combine flour and salt in medium bowl; gradually add to butter mixture. Reserve 2 cups dough. Beat chocolate into dough in bowl until smooth. Cover both doughs and refrigerate until firm enough to handle, about 20 minutes.

Preheat oven to 400°F. Roll out vanilla dough between two sheets of waxed paper to ½-inch thickness. Cut into 5×4-inch rectangles. Place chocolate dough on sheet of waxed paper. Using waxed paper to hold dough, roll back and forth to form a log about 1 inch in diameter. Cut into 5-inch-long logs. Place chocolate log in center of vanilla rectangle. Wrap vanilla dough around log and fit into cookie press fitted with star disc. Press dough onto ungreased cookie sheets 1½ inches apart. Bake about 10 minutes or until just set. Remove cookies with spatula to wire racks; cool completely.

Makes about 4 dozen cookies

Chocolate Spritz

2 squares (1 ounce each) unsweetened
   chocolate
1 cup butter, softened
½ cup granulated sugar
1 egg
1 teaspoon vanilla
¼ teaspoon salt
2¼ cups all-purpose flour
   Powdered sugar

Preheat oven to 400°F. Line cookie sheets with parchment paper or leave ungreased. Melt chocolate in top of double boiler over hot, not boiling, water. Remove from heat; cool. Beat butter, granulated sugar, egg, vanilla and salt in large bowl until light. Blend in melted chocolate and flour until stiff. Fit cookie press with your choice of plate. Load press with dough; press cookies out onto cookie sheets, spacing 2 inches apart.

Bake 5 to 7 minutes or just until very slightly browned around edges. Remove to wire racks to cool. Sprinkle with powdered sugar.

Makes about 5 dozen cookies

Checkerboard Bars

  ½ cup hazelnuts (2½ ounces)
  4 ounces bittersweet or semisweet chocolate
    candy bar, broken into pieces
2¼ cups all-purpose flour
  ½ teaspoon baking powder
  ¼ teaspoon salt
  ¾ cup butter or margarine, softened
  ¾ cup sugar
  2 eggs, divided
  1 teaspoon vanilla

Preheat oven to 350°F. To remove skins from hazelnuts, spread hazelnuts in single layer on baking sheet. Bake 10 to 12 minutes or until toasted and skins begin to flake off; let cool slightly. Wrap hazelnuts in heavy kitchen towel; rub against towel to remove as much of the skins as possible. Place hazelnuts in food processor; process until finely chopped, but not pasty.

Melt chocolate in small bowl over very hot water, stirring until smooth. Set aside.

Combine flour, baking powder and salt in medium bowl. Beat butter and sugar in large bowl with electric mixer at medium speed until light and fluffy. Beat in 1 egg and vanilla. Gradually add flour mixture; beat well.

Reserve 1¼ cups dough. Stir melted chocolate and chopped hazelnuts into remaining dough. Wrap both doughs in plastic wrap and refrigerate 20 minutes.

Unwrap and roll out chocolate dough on lightly floured surface to ⅓-inch thickness with floured rolling pin. Cut dough into eight 4×¾-inch strips. Reroll scraps as necessary, until all dough has been cut into strips. Repeat process with vanilla dough.

To assemble, beat remaining 1 egg in small bowl. Place one strip of chocolate dough on sheet of plastic wrap. Brush edge with egg. Place one strip of vanilla dough next to chocolate dough. Brush edge with egg. Repeat with one more chocolate strip and one more vanilla strip to make bottom layer. Brush top with egg.

Prepare second row by stacking strips on first row, alternating vanilla dough over chocolate and chocolate over vanilla dough. Brush edge of each strip and top layer with egg. Repeat with third row to complete 1 checkerboard bar. Repeat entire process with remaining dough strips to complete second checkerboard bar. Cover with plastic wrap; refrigerate 1 hour or until firm enough to slice.

Preheat oven to 350°F. Grease cookie sheets. Cut checkerboard bar crosswise with long, sharp knife into ¼-inch slices. Place 2 inches apart on prepared cookie sheets.

Bake 10 to 12 minutes or until set. Cool cookies on cookie sheets 2 minutes. Remove cookies with spatula to wire racks; cool completely. Store tightly covered at room temperature or freeze up to 3 months.   *Makes 2 dozen bars*

Watermelon Slices

> 1 package DUNCAN HINES® Golden Sugar Cookie Mix
> 1 egg
> ¼ cup CRISCO® Oil or CRISCO® PURITAN® Canola Oil
> 1½ tablespoons water
> 12 drops red food coloring
> 5 drops green food coloring
> Chocolate sprinkles

1. Combine cookie mix, egg, oil and water in large bowl. Stir until thoroughly blended; reserve ⅓ cup dough.

2. For red cookie dough, combine remaining dough with red food coloring. Stir until evenly tinted. On waxed paper, shape dough into 12-inch-long roll with one side flattened. Cover; refrigerate with flat side down until firm.

3. For green cookie dough, combine reserved ⅓ cup dough with green food coloring in small bowl. Stir until evenly tinted. Place between 2 layers of waxed paper. Roll dough into 12×4-inch rectangle. Refrigerate 15 minutes. Preheat oven to 375°F.

4. To assemble, remove green dough rectangle from refrigerator. Remove top layer of waxed paper. Trim edges along both 12-inch sides. Remove red dough log from refrigerator. Place red dough log, flattened side up, along center of green dough. Mold green dough up to edge of flattened side of red dough. Remove bottom layer of waxed paper. Trim excess green dough, if necessary.

Watermelon Slices

5. Cut chilled roll, flat side down, into ¼-inch-thick slices with sharp knife. Place slices 2 inches apart on ungreased baking sheets. Sprinkle chocolate sprinkles on red dough for seeds. Bake at 375°F for 7 minutes or until set. Cool 1 minute on baking sheets. Remove to cooling racks. Cool completely. Store between layers of waxed paper in airtight container.

Makes 3 to 4 dozen cookies

Cappuccino Bon Bons

> 1 package DUNCAN HINES® Chocolate Lovers'
> Fudge Brownie Mix, Family Size
> 2 eggs
> ⅓ cup water
> ⅓ cup CRISCO® Oil or CRISCO® PURITAN®
> Canola Oil
> 1½ tablespoons FOLGERS® Instant Coffee
> 1 teaspoon ground cinnamon
> Whipped topping
> Cinnamon

1. Preheat oven to 350°F. Place 2-inch foil cupcake liners on cookie sheet.

2. Combine brownie mix, eggs, water, oil, instant coffee and cinnamon. Stir with spoon until well blended, about 50 strokes. Fill each cupcake liner with 1 measuring tablespoon batter. Bake 12 to 15 minutes or until wooden toothpick inserted in center comes out clean. Cool completely. Garnish with whipped topping and a dash of cinnamon. Refrigerate until ready to serve. *Makes about 40 bon bons*

Tip: *To make larger Bon Bons, use twelve 2½-inch foil cupcake liners and fill with ¼ cup batter. Bake 28 to 30 minutes.*

Mini Pecan Tarts

TART SHELLS
> 2 cups all-purpose flour
> 1 teaspoon granulated sugar
> Pinch of salt
> 1½ sticks cold butter or margarine,
> cut into pieces
> ⅓ cup ice water

FILLING
> 1 cup powdered sugar
> ½ cup butter or margarine
> ⅓ cup dark corn syrup
> 1 cup chopped pecans
> 36 pecan halves

For tart shells, combine flour, granulated sugar and salt in large bowl. Using pastry blender or two knives, cut butter into dry ingredients until mixture resembles coarse corn meal. Add water, 1 tablespoon at a time, kneading mixture until dough forms a ball. Wrap dough in plastic wrap, flatten and refrigerate at least 30 minutes.

Preheat oven to 375°F. Grease mini-muffin pans. Roll out dough on lightly floured surface to ⅛-inch thickness. Cut out 3-inch circles using cookie cutter; press into prepared mini-muffin cups and bake about 8 minutes or until very lightly browned. Remove from oven. *Reduce oven temperature to 350°F.*

For filling, combine powdered sugar, ½ cup butter and corn syrup in 2-quart saucepan. Cook over medium heat, stirring occasionally, until mixture comes to a full boil, 4 to 5 minutes. Remove from heat; stir in chopped pecans. Spoon into warm baked shells. Top each with a pecan half. Bake 5 minutes. Cool completely; remove from pans. *Makes 3 dozen tarts*

Apricot-Pecan Tassies

PASTRY
- 1 cup all-purpose flour
- ½ cup butter, cut into pieces
- 6 tablespoons light cream cheese

FILLING
- ¾ cup packed light brown sugar
- 1 egg, lightly beaten
- 1 tablespoon butter, softened
- ½ teaspoon vanilla
- ¼ teaspoon salt
- ⅔ cup California dried apricot halves, diced (about 4 ounces)
- ⅓ cup chopped pecans

For Pastry, combine flour, ½ cup butter and cream cheese in food processor; process until dough forms a ball and cleans sides of bowl. Wrap in plastic wrap; chill 15 minutes.

For Filling, preheat oven to 325°F. In large bowl, combine brown sugar, egg, 1 tablespoon butter, vanilla and salt; beat until smooth. Stir in apricots and pecans.

Shape dough into 1-inch balls; place each in paper-lined or greased miniature muffin cup or tart pan. Press dough on bottom and up side of each cup; fill each with 1 teaspoon filling.

Bake 25 minutes or until golden and filling is set. Cool in pans on wire racks. Cookies can be wrapped tightly in plastic and frozen up to six weeks. *Makes 24 cookies*

Favorite recipe from **California Apricot Advisory Board**

Apricot-Pecan Tassies

Chocolate-Topped Linzer Cookies

3 cups hazelnuts, toasted, skins removed, divided (see page 226)
1 cup unsalted butter, softened
1 cup powdered sugar, sifted
½ teaspoon grated lemon peel
¼ teaspoon salt
½ egg*
3 cups sifted all-purpose flour
½ cup nougat paste**
½ cup seedless red raspberry jam
6 squares (1 ounce each) semisweet chocolate
2 tablespoons shortening

*To measure ½ egg, lightly beat 1 egg in glass measuring cup; remove half for use in recipe.

**Nougat paste, a mixture of ground hazelnuts, sugar and semisweet chocolate is available in specialty candy and gourmet food shops. If unavailable, substitute melted semisweet chocolate to attach cookie layers.

Place 1½ cups hazelnuts in food processor or blender; process until finely ground. (You should have ½ cup ground nuts; if necessary, process more nuts.) Set aside remaining whole nuts for garnish.

Beat butter, sugar, lemon peel and salt in large bowl until thoroughly blended. Do not overmix. Add ½ egg; beat until well mixed. Stir in ground hazelnuts. Gradually stir in flour. Divide dough into quarters. Wrap each portion; refrigerate until firm, about 2 hours.

Preheat oven to 350°F. Line cookie sheets with parchment paper. Roll out dough, one quarter at a time, ⅛ to ¹⁄₁₆ inch thick on floured pastry cloth. Cut out with 1¼-inch round cutter. Place ¾ inch apart on prepared cookie sheets.

Bake 7 to 8 minutes or until lightly browned. Let cookies cool completely on cookie sheets set on wire racks. Spoon nougat paste into pastry bag fitted with ¼-inch round tip. Pipe about ¼ teaspoon paste onto centers of ⅓ of cookies. Top with plain cookies; press gently.

Spoon raspberry jam into pastry bag fitted with ⅓-inch round tip. Pipe about ⅓ teaspoon jam onto centers of second cookie layers. Top with plain cookies; press gently. Let cookies stand about 1 hour.

Melt chocolate and shortening in small, heavy saucepan over low heat, stirring until smooth. Press cookie layers lightly together. Dip top of each cookie into chocolate mixture just to cover. Shake to remove excess chocolate. Place cookies, chocolate side up, on wire racks; press reserved whole hazelnuts into soft chocolate in centers of cookies. Let stand until chocolate is set.   *Makes about 4 dozen cookies*

Acknowledgments

The publishers would like to thank the companies and organizations listed below for the use of their recipes and photographs in this publication.

Best Foods, a Division of CPC International Inc.

Blue Diamond Growers

Borden Kitchens, Borden, Inc.

California Apricot Advisory Board

Dole Food Company, Inc.

Hershey Foods Corporation

Kahlúa Liqueur

Kellogg Company

Kraft Foods, Inc.

Leaf®, Inc.

M&M/Mars

MOTT'S® U.S.A., a division of Cadbury Beverages Inc.

Nabisco Foods Group

National Cherry Foundation

National Honey Board

Nestlé Food Company

Oregon Washington California Pear Bureau

The Procter & Gamble Company

The Quaker Oats Company

Roman Meal Company

Sokol and Company

USA Rice Council

Wisconsin Milk Marketing Board

Index

METRIC CONVERSION CHART

VOLUME MEASUREMENTS (dry)

1/8 teaspoon = 0.5 mL
1/4 teaspoon = 1 mL
1/2 teaspoon = 2 mL
3/4 teaspoon = 4 mL
1 teaspoon = 5 mL
1 tablespoon = 15 mL
2 tablespoons = 30 mL
1/4 cup = 60 mL
1/3 cup = 75 mL
1/2 cup = 125 mL
2/3 cup = 150 mL
3/4 cup = 175 mL
1 cup = 250 mL
2 cups = 1 pint = 500 mL
3 cups = 750 mL
4 cups = 1 quart = 1 L

VOLUME MEASUREMENTS (fluid)

1 fluid ounce (2 tablespoons) = 30 mL
4 fluid ounces (1/2 cup) = 125 mL
8 fluid ounces (1 cup) = 250 mL
12 fluid ounces (1 1/2 cups) = 375 mL
16 fluid ounces (2 cups) = 500 mL

WEIGHTS (mass)

1/2 ounce = 15 g
1 ounce = 30 g
3 ounces = 90 g
4 ounces = 120 g
8 ounces = 225 g
10 ounces = 285 g
12 ounces = 360 g
16 ounces = 1 pound = 450 g

DIMENSIONS

1/16 inch = 2 mm
1/8 inch = 3 mm
1/4 inch = 6 mm
1/2 inch = 1.5 cm
3/4 inch = 2 cm
1 inch = 2.5 cm

OVEN TEMPERATURES

250°F = 120°C
275°F = 140°C
300°F = 150°C
325°F = 160°C
350°F = 180°C
375°F = 190°C
400°F = 200°C
425°F = 220°C
450°F = 230°C

BAKING PAN SIZES

Utensil	Size in Inches/Quarts	Metric Volume	Size in Centimeters
Baking or	8×8×2	2 L	20×20×5
Cake Pan	9×9×2	2.5 L	22×22×5
(square or	12×8×2	3 L	30×20×5
rectangular)	13×9×2	3.5 L	33×23×5
Loaf Pan	8×4×3	1.5 L	20×10×7
	9×5×3	2 L	23×13×7
Round Layer	8×1½	1.2 L	20×4
Cake Pan	9×1½	1.5 L	23×4
Pie Plate	8×1¼	750 mL	20×3
	9×1¼	1 L	23×3
Baking Dish	1 quart	1 L	—
or Casserole	1½ quart	1.5 L	—
	2 quart	2 L	—